STAYING
THE
COURSE

STAYING
THE
COURSE

How Unflinching Dedication and Persistence
Have Built a Successful Private College in a
Region of Isolation and Poverty

ALICE W. BROWN

authorHOUSE®

AuthorHouse™LLC
1663 Liberty Drive
Bloomington, IN 47403
www.authorhouse.com
Phone: 1-800-839-8640

Published by AuthorHouse   12/26/2013

ISBN: 978-1-4918-2107-7 (sc)
ISBN: 978-1-4918-2106-0 (e)

Library of Congress Control Number: 2013917743

CONTENTS

PREFACE

These days it is hard to find an issue of *The Chronicle of Higher Education* or *Inside Higher Ed* that doesn't include a story or at least a note about a college that is facing financial difficulties that threaten the very existence of the institution. Recently, articles covered financial woes leading to the closing of three colleges: Saint Paul's College in Lawrenceville, Virginia; University of Northern Virginia in Annandale, Virginia; and Chancellor U (once Myers University) in Seven Hill, Ohio.[1] Another story was about a college facing the loss of accreditation as a result of money problems. Three of these four colleges have histories of over 100 years.

A quick look at a list of all colleges that have closed[2] indicates the characteristics most common for such institutions are (1) a rural location, (2) a denominational affiliation and (3) a mission of service to the disadvantaged. Another article in *The Chronicle* about the continuing declines in net revenues for colleges says the pressures today are "concentrated in colleges that are small, draw students from a narrow demographic and geographic pool, and are less-selective in admissions . . . ."[3] Yet, despite the publicity drawn to the stories about failing colleges, there are many others that face the same threats from external and internal sources as those that closed but continue to move forward.

Those thriving seem most often to be ones with large endowments, affluent students, and the resources of wealthy alumni and other benefactors. This book is about Cumberland College (also known as the University of the Cumberlands) in Kentucky, a college with all the threats facing institutions of higher education and few of the advantages elite colleges have. What is remarkable about this particular college is that despite its rural location, its strong ties to a conservative denomination, and its commitment to serving financially poor students, it has managed to build a stable, sustainable financial base.

A number of colleges once considered endangered have been able to "turn around" by merging with another campus or by borrowing large sums of money to revamp their campuses to attract students who do not require financial aid. Cumberland College has all, or at least most, of the traits of colleges that are barely surviving or have closed; but, unlike some such colleges, it has never rejected its original mission in the process of strengthening its financial base. It continues to hold firm to a belief in and a commitment to serve the Appalachian region and its people.

Despite its disadvantages, Cumberland stands strong in the network of private liberal arts colleges as it celebrates its history of 125 years. The institution continues to operate with a secure financial base because it has been patient but persistent as well as entrepreneurial in working toward worthy goals. UC has remained true to the mission defined by its founders while expanding services and offering new academic programs that have strengthened the financial underpinnings of the College. In short, by offering online and graduate degrees programs, the University of the Cumberlands has strengthened the residential, liberal arts Cumberland College.

The University of the Cumberlands (UC) was incorporated as Williamsburg Institute in April 1888 by the Kentucky state legislature to offer the Bachelor of Science, the Bachelor of Arts and the Master of Arts. The institute became Cumberland College in 1913 and reverted to offering two-year degrees until 1959 when it began offering the Bachelor's degree again.[4] In 2005, the College became the University of the Cumberlands. The original intent of this change was that the undergraduate on-campus program would retain the name Cumberland College, and the graduate and online degree programs would reflect the university status. However, most people familiar with the institution use the names interchangeably. In this book, I have used both names, but I have tried to use Cumberland College when referring to past events at the College or policies and practices impacting primarily the undergraduate campus program and University of the Cumberlands or UC when talking about present events or about the full institution incorporating all programs, practices and policies.

The institution is defined in various places as a comprehensive university and in others as a comprehensive college; it is always clear that both are denominationally affiliated with the Kentucky Baptist Convention.

Throughout its history the College has not compromised its principles (even when those principles were not popular in the contemporary culture), and it has faced one of the greatest obstacles to prosperity for small private colleges: location in one of the poorest, most isolated regions of the nation—eastern Kentucky. There are few in the region who can make significant financial contributions to the College even though they see how it benefits the surrounding communities and citizens. The graduates generally find employment in non-profit organizations; they become teachers and social workers or return home to care for families that are committed to the region and where the only jobs available are low-paying ones. Almost 100 percent of those who choose to attend the College need significant financial aid to do so, and few of the graduates can afford to make large financial contributions to their alma mater despite the fact that most are very grateful for the opportunity to attend the College.

In the book written about the rise of Elon University, a poster child for "turnaround colleges," the author, George Keller, laments, ". . . American scholars of higher education have seldom ventured to study in detail a single institution's policies, plans, people, and progress. Micro studies to investigate how one college or university conducts itself are extremely rare."[5] The response of the current president of Cumberland to the idea of writing a book about the College was that "little has been written about the small college . . . . It continues to be shrouded in mystery . . . ."[6] Perhaps the book that focused most attention on such institutions—those I have heard referred to as being "well thought of but not thought of very often"—is *The Invisible College* by Alexander Astin and Calvin Lee, and that book was first published in the early 1970s. These days it is rare for the press or other media to focus a story on the positive aspects of a small college. It is even rarer for a book about such colleges to be popular.

Because so little attention has been paid to the small residential colleges working hard to help generations of disadvantaged students move to a level of financial security many thought they would never know, it seems appropriate to focus attention on one such college to identify those characteristics and actions that have made it possible for the College to grow and remain strong over years of economic crises across the nation. *Transforming a College*, the book written by Keller about Elon, had a strong reception and has continued to attract attention, but that transformation was based on significant borrowing to renovate the campus and major recruiting to attract wealthy students not in need of financial aid. By looking at a college that has thrived by honoring its original mission of service to the poor while taking advantage of new methods of course delivery to attract additional populations, perhaps colleges striving to survive can learn other ways to make a college sustainable. Such information is especially relevant today when "private universities without national recognition and large endowments are at great financial risk."[7] Certainly UC is not the only denominational college in a rural area dedicated to serving poor students. It is just one of the best examples of a college that has learned how to thrive in a national environment that seems increasingly hostile to such institutions.

This book was never intended to be a scholarly study of the College; it is simply a collection of personal reflections about the secrets of the success of one small college. Obviously, it is impossible to detail in one book all the aspects of operations and life that make the University what it is. Any attempt to reflect the qualities—tangible and intangible—that have established and sustained Cumberland College over its 125-year history would be woefully inadequate. An entire book could be written on the role of service programs, athletics, online courses—or on any one of the many aspects that have contributed to making and keeping the College strong. The goal for this book is to illustrate that with dedicated and entrepreneurial leadership, generous people with financial resources and talented faculty and staff focused on the needs of students, a college can build a solid financial base and a strong academic reputation regardless of the multiple obstacles that have to be overcome. This book points out some of the major programs and approaches that have given UC a noticeable measure of its success and are ones that could be replicated by other small colleges struggling to build financial security at the same time they build a reputation for integrity and a quality curriculum. Other colleges can compare their leadership, finances and culture to those of UC to see where UC might serve as a guide to a better future. In addition to information about UC, references are included that the current president has found useful in his more than three decades of leading the College.

Oliver Wendell Holmes Jr. advises: ". . . All the use of life is in specific solutions, which cannot be reached through generalities any more than a picture can be painted by knowing some rules of method. They are reached by insight, tact, and specific knowledge."[8] This book offers specific solutions one college has identified as its pathway to a successful future.

CHAPTER 1: REGION

The University of the Cumberlands is located in Whitley County, in the middle of the Cumberland Mountains with elevations as high as 2,220 feet. The county holds the largest waterfall in Kentucky, the beautiful Cumberland Falls State Resort Park, and 38,000 acres of preserved land in the Daniel Boone National Forest. Yet the beauty of the region and its natural resources are not generally the focus when people refer to this part of Appalachia.

Whitley County, home of UC, is seldom the focus of national news, but when it is the stories are almost invariably ones criticizing the local culture. The weekly *60 Minutes* television show once covered the story of a local superintendent of schools who had hired some 200 of his relatives—a story uncovered by Ernie Harris, a graduate of UC. A more recent *60 Minutes* program focused on the story of a young journalist who, at that time, was a student at UC and was working for the *Times-Tribune* in nearby Corbin, Kentucky. The student, Adam Sulfridge, and his editor at the paper were able to do what the FBI had failed to do in years of trying: they exposed the Whitley County sheriff who, during his roughly eight years in office, had accepted money and other goods in exchange for allowing local criminals to go free. The sheriff was sentenced to 15.5 years in federal prison and a local lawyer was sentenced to three years for a variety of crimes, including drug trafficking, money laundering, and extorting money from those accused of criminal activities.[1] On a visit I made to the College in 2012, headlines in a local paper read "14 Arrested in Drug Roundup" and "$1,000 Reward Offered for Robbery Info." On another trip, the lead story in a local paper was "A Dozen Dealers Targeted in Latest Whitley Drug Raid."[2] Such news reports and television shows like the *Dukes of Hazard* and, more recently, *Justified,* portray a region rife with crime, corruption, and conspiracies.

Perhaps the most noticeable characteristic of the region is not crime but poverty. The 2010 census indicated a population of 35,637—not many above the 1920 census report of 31,982 and 200 fewer than the 2000 census data. In Williamsburg itself, the population was 5,245. It is no surprise that across the isolated county only about 2 percent of the population is minorities, including African Americans, Asians, and Hispanics.[3] The median income for a family in the last census was $27,871 with males having a median income of almost $10,000 more than females. The per capita income was $12,777 with over a quarter of the population living below the poverty line. Only about 70 percent of those 25 and older have graduated from high school and only 12 percent in that age bracket have a bachelor's degree or higher.[4] Some reports reflect the seriousness of poverty in the area by reporting figures related to "extreme poverty" where household incomes are "below 50 percent of the poverty threshold . . . . By the end of 2009, almost one in ten people in Mississippi was in extreme poverty—the nation's highest rate." Kentucky was second in the nation with 8 percent in extreme poverty.[5]

In an article published in late 2012, Thomas Miller, who has worked to address the problems of the Appalachian region for over 40 years, expresses what has become the frustration of a lot of people: ". . . We have tried it all: fifty years of economic development involving lots and lots of taxpayer money, large scale and small spending on one program after another, from roads to hospitals, from venture capital to industrial sites, job training to craft cooperatives, Foxfire to clean coal. Yet our economy remains woefully deficient and poised to fall into an even bigger sinkhole as our reachable coal reserves play out at the same time that coal is losing favor as a source of energy."[6] He points out that despite the fact that there are many communities that have transformed themselves from poverty to wealth, none seem to offer lessons relevant for the poorest sections of Appalachia.

Certainly the Appalachian Regional Commission has brought some economic revitalization to the region, but the great majority of that success is evident only in the large cities, such as Knoxville and Atlanta. And that fact reflects Miller's conclusion: ". . . Economies do much better in places of higher human density . . . . Skilled and ambitious people quickly move to places best suited to pursue their dreams" and that place has not been

Appalachia. Even those reared in Appalachia who are financially successful as a result of their creativity and entrepreneurship most often became so by moving out of the region. Miller continues, ". . . A certain population density is necessary before you can accumulate the necessary amenities to attract new residents and build the skills and connections between people that can lead to a diversified economy . . . ."[7]

Despite the poor economy of the region and the sparse population, UC continues to provide opportunities to the people of it with enduring hope that better days are ahead. One response to this description of the region was, "If you think it's bad now, what would it be without the heroic efforts by doctors, attorneys, teachers, etc. to improve communities seeking to break the bonds of poverty to become enlightened productive, taxpaying citizens."[8] What would the region be like without the colleges that produced the doctors, lawyers, teachers, etc.? The importance of education to alleviating such serious poverty is reflected by the fact that nationally "only 1.9 percent of all adults with a Bachelor's degree or higher were in extreme poverty in 2009."[9]

When the world hears about Whitley County, it is usually because of political corruption or because of its extreme poverty and bleak future, but it is hard to overlook the beauty of the landscape and the many good people there who are committed to their families and a rural lifestyle. In Whitley County, the Daniel Boone National Forest protects almost 40,000 acres of forest land so there is scenic beauty almost everywhere, and the county is easily accessible by Interstate 75 and U.S. Route 25W. But the natural beauty and good highways have not brought much new tourism or many new industries into that part of the state; coal and timber have remained the primary industries for generations. Local gardens dot the countryside, but the terrain is too rough for farming on a large scale.

One beacon of light in these hills is the College—which rises out of the surrounding environment of decaying buildings and dust-covered vehicles to brighten the landscape with beautiful brick buildings trimmed in white, many topped with cupolas and steeples. But it is not just improvements in the view of the landscape and excellent educational experiences that the College offers. The institution realizes that the surrounding community is critical to the growth of any college. A report by a local newspaper points out how much the financial stability of the community depends on the financial stability of the College. The occupational tax paid to the county by employees of the College was $123,476 in 2012; figures for taxes paid on homes and other property were not included. The College outsources its security, food service, and maintenance, and bookstore services to companies who also employ local residents—who pay city and county taxes. Students spend money locally, as do their parents and friends who come from outside the county to visit.[10]

When the College buys local property, the amount paid the county for building permits is often more than the property might bring the county in taxes for decades, and the college often widens streets, adds sidewalks, replaces water and sewer systems and constructs traffic signs at no cost to the city. In addition, the construction projects provide employment for local residents and for workers who come from other areas to the benefit of local businesses and the occupational tax coffers. And purchases the College makes of properties each year help to keep all local property values at a steady level. The College purchases utilities (water and sewer services), pays for garbage service and pays a hotel/restaurant tax on income from its inn. Last year that total was $340,000.[11] If a certain level of "human density" is critical for the growth of a region, no other business or organization is providing so much of that element for Whitley County as UC.

CHAPTER 2: LEADERSHIP

Trustees should (1) expect to be kept informed about the progress of the institution on at least a monthly basis, (2) take the time to reflect on information received, and (3) make their reactions clear verbally or in writing. They should hire a president with an obvious (and documented) commitment to the region and/or institution and a lot of energy and enthusiasm for the causes he or she pursues and whose spouse can not only inspire but also fulfill some of the president's responsibilities for staying in touch with constituents. The president should select major administrators who have a tie to the region or to a similar region so relating to the culture of the institution and its people is a natural instinct; provide incentives that recognize hard work and dedication; and quickly dismiss or reassign any who clearly do not well fit the role to which they have been assigned.

Trustees

Perhaps the Cumberland College trustees should first be congratulated for selecting James Harold Taylor to follow two long-serving presidents in leading the institution. When Belle Wheelan, president of SACS, was asked to comment on what she thought contributed to the strength of UC, her response referred to the "stability of leadership" at the College, where "the governing board and Dr. Taylor have worked together for many years to ensure needed resources for the university."[1] Often it is especially hard to follow someone who has been a strong force for an institution and to sustain his or her initiatives as well as to carve your own ideas and character into the institution. But Taylor, when he was called to the presidency, had been at the College for a number of years, working in the advancement and other offices; he knew the problems he would be facing as well as the strengths of the institution where he had been a student as well as an employee. Despite strong competition for the position, the trustees knew that Taylor would move the College forward with great strides in ways other candidates were unlikely to do, and he would drive the institution while honoring its mission.

The College has always had trustees committed to the institution, in many cases because they are from the region and know its need for quality educational resources. As Taylor says, **"Cumberland is one of few colleges formed by local people in the coal mining industry to serve their own people and communities . . . ."**[2] In other cases, trustees are identified through their link to the denominational affiliation of the College and their belief in the importance of a Christian education for a stable society.

The chairperson of the current board is Jim Oaks, who served with CSX Transportation as a division superintendent in Corbin from 1977 until 1985 and then in Lexington, Kentucky, as Assistant Vice President of Coal Development until he retired in 1999. He became involved with the Cumberland board when he was based in Corbin, attended the First Baptist Church, and met three people who were then on that board. He has served continuously ever since with the exception of the years between terms when he was required to be an honorary trustee.

According to the Bylaws of the College, members of the board are responsible for "establishing institutional policies, securing financial resources to support adequately the University's program, and selecting and evaluating the President of the University. The Board shall not be subject to undue outside pressures nor allow the administration to be subjected to undue outside pressures. The Board shall have the ultimate control over the structure and content of all academic programs of the University as well as the business, fiscal and other affairs of the University." At UC the board is composed of 28 trustees and the president who serves without vote. At least nine must be residents of the local county, and no more than eight may be residents of states outside Kentucky. Each trustees is elected to a four-year term but may be reappointed after a one-year period, during which he or she can serve as an honorary member of the board without voice or vote. As a result, currently two of the trustees have provided continuity by serving on the board since the 1970s, before Taylor became president, and seven have come to the board in the last four years. Taylor submits nominees to the Kentucky Baptist Convention for ratification.

Members bring various experiences and expertise to the board: there are several with financial acumen gained through professional positions with banks or major businesses; several with strong knowledge about the state and federal government operations; a judge; and an architectural engineer. All have skills important to serving the College—including the ability to make the hard decisions that go with managing a college's operating budget. Last year, for example, insurance costs increased 20 percent and such increases are expected to continue. This year the board had to deal with a cut in the contribution expected from the Kentucky Baptist Convention. Board members help with the critical fund-raising necessary to sustain the College by talking about it to friends and by recommending to Taylor people he should visit as perspective donors. They serve to represent the College in areas where they live and where they work. In Oaks words, "I have served on a lot of boards, but I have never served with a better board; they understand the needs of the school and are very supportive of its president. They ask important and pointed questions but have almost always approved my recommendations."[3]

There are a number of committees appointed by the board chair and composed of members of the board: Academic Affairs; Finance, Budget and Investment (FBI); Student Services; Honorary Degrees; Buildings and Grounds; Stewardship; Land Development, and Executive. Each trustee serves on two of the committees, and they all make financial contributions even though there are no required minimum levels of giving. Currently four of the trustees are ministers but generally there are more on the board—and, for obvious reasons, ministers are seldom in a position to make major financial contributions even to worthy organizations affiliated with their own denomination. The full board meets in person twice a year; the Executive and Finance Committees meet more often if needed.

Perhaps the most important role all board members serve is selecting and supporting a president they can trust to carry out their policies and represent them and the College to the general public in positive ways. The attitude of the UC board toward the current president was expressed by one who has served as a trustee at a nearby college: "The board of Cumberland has confidence in Taylor's judgment and does not try to micromanage him; like him, they believe in the mission of the College and value efforts to sustain it."[4] A major complaint of many college presidents is about boards that micromanage, but micromanagement does not ever seem to have been a problem for the president of UC.

The responsibilities of the board, as Taylor outlined them for SACS, are:

Being an aggressive advocate for the college in recruiting students, raising money and spreading goodwill;

Bringing the same love and devotion to the college one brings to one's own business;

Attending Board meetings and keeping informed;

Reviewing the fiscal, physical and academic needs and entering into meaningful dialogue;

Being familiar with the college Policies and Procedures;

Helping to develop friends by literally bringing the prospective donors to the Lodge and by literally bringing prospective students to the campus;

Helping get the college planned gifts and in Wills, especially in the Wills of people who have no children;

Helping attract friends, funds and freshmen;

Bringing wit, wealth and wisdom to the Board, and hopefully by making Cumberland College the fourth most important thing in our lives following: a. Our faith; b. Our family; c. Our work.[5]

Typically 50 percent of the trustees are alumni or alumnae of the College, and for these folks, keeping a realistic eye on the current situations the institution faces and separating those views from their memories of times past can be difficult. As Taylor says, **"Alumni remember a time that never was with the greatest accuracy."**[6] Many seem to think that if a college could keep everything as it once was, it would have no problems. Fortunately, alums on the UC board seem to realize that times have changed since their college days, and reactions and responses to various issues must change as well.

Generally, the most important ally a college president can have (outside of family) is the chair of the board. The relationship between Taylor and his board chairs has been so strong that when asked if he wants to consult with the chair on an important issue to consider what the chair thinks, his response is often, **"I don't usually have to ask what my Chairman thinks. I generally know what my Chairman thinks. If you are a president and have to ask, you are in trouble."**[7] Of course, the reverse is also true: the chair should always know what the president thinks.

To help assure the board is always well informed, Taylor, with his staff, sends monthly reports to each trustee, and he speak frequently with the chair to insure that as president he knows that particular person's thoughts on all the issues; Taylor knows that keeping communications open is important. All the updates and communications keep the trustees informed so they can make suggestions or, at the very least, not be surprised by a comment made at a local event or in the press about something at the College or at the next board meeting. He also understands that what the trustees want to know is not the problems that exist but the solutions. They especially want to hear about the accomplishments of the College and those on the campus. As he says, **"Trustees want to feel the pride of association or affiliation and to have bragging rights."**[8] In advising new presidents, Taylor reminds them, **"Board meetings should be celebrations, not hand-wringing events."**[9]

The agenda for a meeting of the trustees is usually predictable: minutes from the previous meeting, approval of budget and items related to it, announcements of new funding, programs and current events, awarding of tenure or other promotions, and periodic reviews of the work of the president. The vice presidents each bring a full report to every board meetings. All materials are sent to the trustees three weeks before a meeting—so there are no surprises. Trustees are encouraged to ask questions and to make observations. The FBI Committee is one of the most active groups. A lot of time is spent with comparative data so that the trustees can see how the College is faring in comparison with its peer and aspirant institutions. It is important that trustees trust the president and his or her staff, but it is equally important that the president and staff verify the information being shared.

Over the years, the trustees at Cumberland have had their share of major crises with which to deal: the spread of community colleges across Kentucky, the expansion of the state public universities through branches opened in the local region, the closing of a neighboring college and its need for assistance in that process, the occasional fall of the value of the endowment as the result of national economic problems, the building and slow development of the Cumberland Inn, a lawsuit by a faculty member who felt he was wrongfully terminated (eventually settled in favor of the College), and the negative publicity wrought by a student who felt the College had discriminated against him. How the trustees handle such matters is generally confidential, but the trustees and president have always been gracious in sharing relevant information with the press and others who have legitimate reasons for inquiring. Suffice it to say that in every case the trustees and the president spoke with one voice to address the problem and move the College forward.

I can testify that such openness is not the case with all colleges. In the course of researching over a dozen colleges for my first two books about how colleges turn themselves around or close, I was frequently told no one was available to talk with me, the information requested was "confidential," or I had "no right to be on the campus." A question which one would assume could be answered by public records, such as "how much money does the institution get from the federal government to help fulfill its obligations," was met with the response, "I'm not at liberty to give you that information." In the case of Cumberland, I have never asked a question, requested permission to see a document, or taped a discussion where I did not feel that those responding were not completely open and honest. It seems that the trustees as well as the president realize the value of being transparent in a world where secrecy is often viewed with suspicion and the truth is generally less harmful than the imagined. As Taylor says, **"No one is smart enough to lie."**[10] He might have added, "and not be caught in the lie."

When Taylor is working with the trustees, he tries to frame the issues and approach them and the resulting decisions with humility, recognizing that the trustees are the final authority. In response, the trustees have addressed the relevant issues in very positive ways. When a nearby college faced closing in the middle of a semester, the trustees offered financial assistance to enable a "teach-out" at that campus so the college could complete the semester and students could receive credit for their courses being taken. When the community colleges and branch campuses of the state institutions proliferated in the region, Cumberland took the position of appreciating the fact that Cumberland would no longer be the college students attend because it is the only one nearby; it would move from being "a college of access" to become "a college of choice."[11] Cumberland eliminated a number of remedial courses, admitted that students needing such courses might be better served by a community college, and focused on recruiting students with strong academic records.

Donald W. Good, who served as Vice President of Academics at UC from 2002 until 2007, after having served in administration at Carson-Newman College in Tennessee from 1989 until 2002, was struck when he was at UC by the good relationship between the Kentucky Baptist Convention and the College. While in Tennessee he sensed hostility between the Church and Carson-Newman, leading to talk about separation of the two. In Kentucky, Good was impressed with "how cordial and constructive the meetings between the Church and College were."[12] The board at UC has never considered separating the institution from the Church; there seems to be, in fact, agreement all around that the two groups are mutually beneficial. The College obviously appreciates the financial support the Convention provides and the fact that Convention members have not tried to interfere with curriculum issues. UC faculty are free to teach issues as they see fit; there are all types of denominations in the classrooms, and there is no requirement for faculty to take an oath of allegiance to any particular church. The roughly $1.3 million that UC has usually received each year from the Convention is clearly important, and even though the University is currently facing the possibility that the contribution will be reduced for 2013-2014, whatever the amount received, it will be significant for the work of the institution.

When Oaks was asked the question about what makes UC special, his answer was similar to Wheelan's:

> The college has a president so understanding of the needs, so honest and such a good spiritual leader, and he has the help of a terrific team

11

because he has the ability to evaluate people he believes in and can trust and is able to delegate responsibilities to them they can fulfill well. The college has good staff, a good reputation, a good curriculum offering different degrees (now including doctoral degrees), strong enforcement of the bylaws and other rules governing the college, and a facility that is unequaled in the area.[13]

(Appendix A contains a list of current trustees.)

President

Nine presidents (not counting 2 interims) have led Cumberland College. This brief statement reflects an important characteristic of many small colleges that seem to be thriving today: few presidents—each with a history documenting a strong commitment to the region and/or the institution prior to becoming president. (See Appendix B for a listing of the presidents of Cumberland College and terms served.) While the simple answer to the question of how long a president should stay in office at one institution is that the president should stay as long as he or she is effective and leave when he or she becomes ineffective, a number of scholars, such as William Bowen, suggest that ten years is probably the length of time a college president can be effective in that role.[14] Others have illustrated that a critical element for colleges that have struggled to maintain financial stability is having presidents who stay long enough to fulfill their personal vision for the college—with each moving the college to a level higher in terms of programs offered and financial security than that of the previous leader.[15] And in most cases, fulfilling a personal vision for a college takes longer than ten years. Again, however, there is no number of years at a college that will assure a president's success at any college.

When I was directing the Appalachian College Association (ACA) from 1983-2008, in each of the five states served by that program there were a number of long-serving presidents who could claim numerous accomplishments at each college served: in Kentucky, Willis Weatherford was the sixth president of Berea College, and he served from 1967 until 1984; in Tennessee, Cordell Maddox was the tenth president at Carson-Newman, serving from 1977 until 2000; in Virginia, Tom Morris served

Emory & Henry from 1992 until 2006 and would probably have served longer had the governor not appointed him to a prominent position in the state's education system; in West Virginia, Ed Welch became president of the University of Charleston in 1989 and remains president today; and in North Carolina, Fred Bentley served from 1966-1996 at Mars Hill College. And under each of those long-serving presidents, his college thrived. None of those listed here can claim the longevity in a presidency that Taylor can, serving from 1980 until today, but they all illustrate characteristics representative of strong presidents at small colleges: fierce belief in mission, hard work to accomplish that mission, and the ability to tell the story of the college often and well. UC has had nine such presidents.

From my research and experience, it seems that so long as a college has a distinguished history, a strong endowment, and an alumni base heavily populated by professionals earning six-figure incomes, presidential transitions are not as traumatic as they can be when a college is teetering between assurance of future prosperity and the threat of lost accreditation. The selection of a president for a heavily endowed, highly selective college does not pose the challenges that selection of a leader for a college that has operated near the edge of financial disaster for decades might. And, from my experience, it seems that new presidents coming to institutions with which they are familiar primarily from print literature invariably underestimate the problems that will face them. Taylor tells the story of asking a trustee from a college, "Do you tell the candidate the truth [about the position of presidency at that college]?" The response was "Heavens, no. We'd never get a president if we were honest."[16] Since Taylor had been a student at the College and the head of development prior to considering the presidency, he came to that position with his "eyes wide open."

When I have interviewed presidents at colleges threatened with foreclosure, loss of accreditation or similar catastrophes, those holding the position often explained that they wanted to be president of the institution because they had held other administrative positions at other colleges and felt they were ready to be at the helm of a college. Bruce Heilman served as president of Meredith College (1966-1971) and president of the University of Richmond (1971-1986 and 1987-1988). He has had multiple experiences in the world of small colleges, including serving on the board of Campbellsville College in Kentucky; as business and financial officer at Kentucky Wesleyan College, Georgetown College in Kentucky and Peabody College in Tennessee; and as a vice president of administration at Peabody. These and other experiences have given him immense insight into the ways such colleges operate and sensitivity to those serving in them. Heilman contributes the success of Cumberland College to the fact that "(1) the college has had a president who has a deep commitment to what the college represents and (2) the college has held firmly to its mission. Taylor did not become president of the college because he wanted to be a president but because he believed in the mission of the college and was willing to devote his life to engaging in it and supporting it."[17] A lot of presidents focus on getting the next job, using the current institution as a stepping stone. Those who are inclined to recruit a president who has experience in that role at another college need to consider that experience as president at one institution does not necessarily qualify someone well for a presidency at a different college.

I am frequently amused to hear a president talk about how he or she "turned around" a college when serving as president for only a year or two. Even if a person can reverse the direction a college might be headed, he or she needs to remain in the president's office for at least six or seven years to be able to state with any assurances that the "turn around" of the college is sustainable. An examination of such colleges as Elon University—a college which is often studied for the lessons it illustrates about changing the direction of an institution—suggests that presidential candidates most likely to help a struggling college thrive are those who have enough of a commitment to the region and/or the specific institution to dedicate the remaining years of their professional lives to that presidency—or to the institution in some form. In the 124 year history of Elon University, there have been eight presidents serving an average of 15.5 years.[18] None served as president at another college before taking that position at Elon, and none left to be president at another college. Each was dedicated to Elon and to serving there as president for as long as he felt he could be a productive leader in that role. The same is true for the nine who have led Cumberland College.

Of those who served Cumberland as president, the early ones often came to the region to serve as ministers and/or faculty at the school and were later called into service as president. Beginning with President Evans in 1919 and including Boswell, who became president in 1947, the men who were asked to be president were from Kentucky until Taylor, who was born in Texas and reared in Michigan although his family was from Kentucky. He moved to Kentucky to attend college at Cumberland.[19]

All Cumberland College presidents have been committed to the region and devoted most of their lives to serving it through the College. They were not men driven by ambition and/or greed to be president. They were men who answered a call that clearly required dedication and commitment to a life of hard work and sacrifice to help students become competent and purposeful citizens. Most of those who accepted this life of the presidency at Cumberland College held the responsibilities for 20 or more years. The first president (then called principal) served only one year before, at age 27, deciding to focus on fund-raising for the College and turning the presidency over to a 28-year-old. The person who followed him, Edwin Ellsworth Wood, served three different terms for a total of 22 years—holding a vice-presidency at the College between his first and second terms and taking a year's vacation after serving 12 years before resuming the responsibilities of president for another seven. Two presidents served terms of four years each in the early history of the College, but since 1925 there have been three presidents: President James Lloyd Creech served 22 years, James Malcolm Boswell served from 1947 until 1980 (33 years), and James Harold Taylor has served since 1980, essentially matching Bowell's tenure and apparently destined to exceed it.

When the president of nearby Alice Lloyd College was asked what he considered the reason UC has maintained a reputation as one of the strongest of the private colleges in Kentucky, his response was the same as that of everyone I asked: "The tremendous leadership of Jim Taylor. He has the longest tenure of any president in Kentucky; he is deeply committed to the mission of the College; he understands the 'nitch' of the College and he has not deviated from it."[20] The focus of this book is the story of the development of the College under Taylor's leadership and the efforts of those who, he readily admits, have helped him. This story reflects efforts to keep the College strong despite the trying times that have challenged small private colleges in the past 30 plus years—and to keep it strong without moving away from its original mission. At the meetings of the ACA presidents, Taylor seldom said much, but when he spoke the other presidents listened. The wisdom that has come from his experiences and dedication deserves to be shared.

From his resume, an article entitled "20 Years of Visionary Leadership," and information he shared during conversations with me, the critical elements of Taylor's story suggest a life of preparation for the presidency. He was born in San Antonio, Texas, in1945; his father was located there during World War II but had been born in Beaver Dam, Kentucky; and Taylor's mother was from Sevierville, Tennessee. After his parents divorced, his mother remarried and Taylor spent most of his youth in Pontiac, Michigan, where his mother, a graduate of Carson-Newman College in Tennessee, worked as an executive secretary for Pontiac Motors and his stepfather worked on the assembly line. His stepfather was of German descent, was hard working, and was strict; he expected the seven children to have jobs early. Taylor shined shoes, sold greeting cards door-to-door, mowed lawns and carried newspapers. In high school he worked in grocery stores; by his senior year he was working eight hours a night loading trucks and boxcars for the Teamsters and United Auto Workers. Still he remained on the honor role throughout his high school years. He had heard of Cumberland College and the fact that many of the students there worked their way through. When he wrote to the College, he received a response from President Boswell saying that if he could pay $700, he could work to cover the rest of the cost of his freshman year. Taylor boarded a bus with the blessing of his parents but the warning from his stepfather that he should "not to come back talking any of that college stuff."

While a student at Cumberland College, Taylor was ordained by the Main Street Baptist Church in 1967; he served as pastor at several churches in Monticello and Williamsburg for a total of just over ten years. Currently, he is a member of the First Baptist Church of Williamsburg.

After graduating with honors from Cumberland in 1968, Taylor stayed at the College to teach speech, argumentation and debate. He served as assistant to the president, director of alumni affairs, director of admissions and director of development. In 1972 he received his master's degree from Union College. In May of 1973 he accepted a position as Vice President for Development at Scarritt College in Nashville,

Tennessee, returning after eight months to Cumberland College to lead the development efforts there. In 1976, he received a doctorate from Nova University SE in Fort Lauderdale, Florida; in 1978, he was named president-elect of Cumberland College; and in August of 1980, he became president of the College. In 1987, he completed the requirements for a second doctorate in education from Peabody College of Vanderbilt University.

Joseph Early, who served with Taylor for 21 years as chief academic officer, tells the story about the transition between Boswell and Taylor. When Taylor was first serving as Boswell's chief fund raiser, Early was teaching at the College. Their two families lived only a few blocks apart and their sons played together. During those years, the two men grew concerned about what they saw as a movement at the College toward making it a Bible College; they feared that under leadership of one of the Baptist ministers they saw lining up to become the next president, the College would cease to maintain a primary focus on the liberal arts. When Taylor left the College to work at Scarritt College, Early began sending his resume to other colleges. When Boswell asked Early why he was unhappy at Cumberland College, the reply was that he feared what would happen under the wrong leadership, that what the College needed was a strong fundraiser as president and that the board should try to bring Taylor back as president. Taylor did return and Boswell announced his retirement and recommended Taylor as the next president in the late fall of 1978. Unfortunately, the appointment was not to take place for roughly 18 months. While most of the faculty were delighted with the announcement, no one anticipated the backlash from the pastors who were expecting to have one of their own become the next president. During the time prior to moving into the presidency, Taylor was bombarded with letters questioning his ability to lead, his loyalty to the College, and even his personal faith. As Taylor was forming his leadership team, he asked Early to be the academic dean, and Early himself became a target of the hate mail. He remembers one letter comparing Taylor and him to John Ehrlichman and H.R Haldeman of Watergate fame—but he never knew whether he was being compared to Ehrlichman or Haldeman.[21] With the support of the trustees, Taylor, at age 33, was named president in the fall of 1980 and took office in early 1981; Early became the academic dean later in 1981.

Taylor's wife agrees that those eighteen months between Boswell's recommendation and the appointment of Taylor to the presidency were rough, but, as she says, "What doesn't kill you makes you stronger," and eventually some of those who made the most vicious attacks became some of Taylor's best supporters.[22] Whatever has made Taylor strong, his strength has served him well as he has moved the College past numerous obstacles despite tight budgets and occasional opposition by entrenched faculty and staff. Knowing the problems that confronted Taylor and some of his appointees helps clarify some of his comments at his installation:

> **I see the first priority in this new day is that of finding consensus, of finding harmony. And consensus or common ground can be found through the planning process. The planning process can enhance relationships among people and can teach us to pull together and to cooperate.**
>
> **So I want to encourage the faculty, students, alumni, and other friends to join in the most sweeping dialogue we've ever had in terms of what we need to do, how we can serve the area and provide quality Christian education, primarily for those students coming from the Appalachia area but also those coming from the plains and valleys, the ocean sides, and the wheat fields.**
>
> **. . . Predicting the future and positioning oneself for the future is not enough. We must be able to shape our destiny and that will be tough in this economy. But I have confidence in our faculty and staff as we move toward our Centennial with vigor. We simply must have the capacity to dream and the ability to make our dreams come true, as presumptuous as that may sound.[23]**

One anonymous source suggested that all the criticisms of those early years left Taylor with a sense of insecurity that he overcame by "out working everyone else." He not only works hard and long, he is incredibly focused on improving the College beyond what even he might have imagined early in his career. Staff accuse him of having "a clean-desk syndrome"; he expects to have his desk cleared at the end of every day, and he expects the same of all the other administrators—an expectation that creates problems for some whose work entails tasks that do not lend themselves to immediate completion. A characteristic that Early pointed out is Taylor's tendency to never forget an idea once it is in his head. If Early was able to present him with data that suggested an idea was not appropriate at the present, he might mentally file the idea away, but he would not forget it.

Taylor frequently says that he spent his first year as president correcting the mistakes of the past president and the next thirty plus years correcting his mistakes.[24] Not many presidents talk about correcting his or her mistakes. And this humility is an important part of Taylor's character. When I commented about seeing his and Dinah's names on the back of a building, he explained that the donors for the building insisted the names be put on the building, so he put them on—the back door. Taylor tries to maintain a low-profile (witness how few pictures there are of him in campus publications) so that others can receive the praise for accomplishments on the campus.

Of the presidents who served as the chair of the board of the ACA when I was leading the organization, Taylor was one of the few who provided me with general advice about leadership. Perhaps the advice I found most surprising was when he asked me, just before his first meeting as the chair of the board of presidents, "So, what's the bad news at the ACA?" When I said, "I don't think I have any," he replied, "Well, if you ever do have bad news, let me deliver it; you want the board to associate you with good news." Apparently, Taylor likes to announce the major gifts received to his board and to have the appropriate vice-presidents announce any litigations, irritations or fiscal frustrations. Still, Taylor is quick to accept responsibility for bad news and give credit to others for the good.

While it is difficult to claim that to be a good college president a person has to have the ability to predict the future, it is good if he or she has the ability to at least understand the direction in which the country seems to be heading. Even in his inauguration speech on May 2, 1981, Taylor seemed to understand the challenges he and the College would face. He referred to the days ahead "when many institutions will witness a downward drift in quality, balance, integrity and character." Those days predicted have arrived.

When asked to speak on "what might happen in the 1980s in private higher education," Taylor explained that even the greatest minds have been unable to forecast a decade ahead such crises as the Vietnam War, the energy crisis, or the economy of scarcity. Still, he was comfortable predicting that the 1980s would see a need to strengthen the values that have made the country great and increasing dissatisfaction with higher education based on what would be viewed as the continuing decline in the quality of education. He endorsed predictions that "After the mid-1980s, with the prolongation of their financial difficulties and the gradual intensification of the battle for students, a growing number of the marginal private institutions in all likelihood may begin to fall by the wayside. One of the momentous consequences may well be the possible liquidation of a good part of private higher education."[25] A study by the American Council of Learned Societies (ACLS) provides the statistics that document the trajectory downward for the private liberal arts sector of higher education:

> As recently as the mid-1950s, the institutions traditionally classified (or self-styled) as liberal arts colleges constituted around 40 percent of the total number of institutions of higher education, and they enrolled about 25 percent of all undergraduates. By the early 1970s they had come to account for only about a quarter of all institutions and enrolled no more than 8 percent of all students. Over the subsequent decades the loss of ground has continued, if at a slower pace . . . . Between 1967 and 1990 some 167 private four-year colleges disappeared, either by closure or by merger.[26]

Even though more students were graduating from the private colleges in the 1980s than in the 1950s, most of the enrollment in institutions of higher education had gone to the public colleges and universities, including the community colleges. And the repeated threat that a number of small private colleges will close must surely cast a cloud over those presidents fighting to build a sustainable base for such schools. A 2011 article on the closing of Lambuth College in Tennessee indicated that "according to information compiled by the U.S. Department of Education, National Center for Education Statistics (NCES), more than 50 private, not-for-profit colleges and universities have closed since 1999."[27] That figure itself suggests that closing is a real possibility for some of the remaining small private colleges in the nation.

In his speech about the future of higher education, after detailing the sad statistics reflecting the disadvantages of the roughly 20 percent of the children in America who live in poverty and the almost constant threat of violence, Taylor stressed the importance of giving people hope for the future—and, in his eyes, much of that hope rests with private higher education. In 1981, Taylor listed worthy objectives for colleges such as Cumberland that are still relevant: (1) a clear vision of purpose, (2) vigorous pursuit of American philanthropy, (3) personalizing services based on individual needs of applicants, and (4) adapting curricula to provide slower learners with the chance to succeed.[28] In reflecting on the importance of instilling moral values as a part of the educational process, Taylor often repeats Theodore Roosevelt's comment: "To educate a person in the mind and not in morals is to educate a menace to society."[29] President Taylor sees it is critical to sustain the benefits most private colleges provide—hope, knowledge, and a strong sense of values.

Taylor attributes one of his favorite quotes to Victor Frankl: "Treat people not the way they are but the way they should be and they will become what they are not. Treat an institution not the way it is, but the way it should be and it will become what it is not."[30] His vision is always clear in his mind, and he knows which goals to set each year to take the College ever closer to fulfilling that vision. But while President Taylor is certainly not a passive man, he is a patient one; he waited many years to see Cumberland clearly on the road to becoming the institution he believed it could and should be. On patience he noted:

> **Always have a series of goals before you which are totally unattainable—lock onto them and pursue them doggedly. Yet I counsel to err on the side of patience. At Cumberland it has taken more than 40 years in development and the presidency to achieve what has been achieved and more must be done. We are only now at the point when clanking radiators and threadbare furniture issues have been addressed.**

Don't focus on the quick fix at the expense of the thoughtful. Consequential thinking required reflection and time.

....

This is a marathon, not a 100 yard sprint.

....

A series of tactics in the overall strategy has allowed us to inch along incrementally. No one activity was monumental, but when taken together, the new buildings, campus expansion and renovation are transformational. We work day in and day out with countless visits, phone calls, direct mail, e-mail and so on.[31]

A person with the reputation for leadership that Taylor has is naturally sought by other colleges looking for a new president. His response has always been that he cannot or will not leave Cumberland. Apparently not even a significant salary increase is an incentive. Once when I saw Taylor's salary in *The Chronicle of Higher Education*, I was surprised at how low it was. I called him and said, "I'm going to stop complaining about my salary as president of the ACA, and start complaining about yours as president of Cumberland." His wife revealed to me that Taylor is not the highest paid person on the campus; that his response to her when she realized this fact was the same as that he had given me: he assured me that he was making plenty of money to allow him and his wife to live comfortably and that there was no point in accumulating more. If there is more money available, he wants to be sure that those working on the campus are well paid and that the needs of the institution are addressed. Clearly Taylor is where he wants to be, doing what he wants to do.

Clark Kerr once wrote:

> The university president in the United States is expected to be a friend of the students, a colleague with the faculty, a good fellow with the alumni, a sound administrator with the trustees, a good speaker with the public, an astute bargainer with the foundations and the federal agencies, a politician with the state legislature, a friend of industry, labor, and agriculture, a persuasive diplomat with donors, a champion of education, a supporter of the professions

(particularly law and medicine), a spokesman to the press, a scholar in his own right, a public servant at the 41 state and national levels, a devotee of football and opera equally, a decent human being, a good husband and father, an active member of the church . . . . No one can be all of these things. Some succeed at being none.[32]

Taylor may not like opera as much as he likes football, but as this book illustrates, he has succeeded in meeting Kerr's expectations regarding the presidency of a college or university in most respects. His hope is that he has been able to handle the presidency "to the extent of having some of the greatest critics giving credit grudgingly. **After all the difference between a politican and a statesman is that the politician has outlived his or her critics**"[33]

Presidential Spouse

As happy as Taylor seems in his role as president, he seems equally happy in his role as husband. I have heard stories for years about how disappointed people often are when President Taylor appears at their doorsteps—without his wife. And I have to admit that I enjoy conversations with Dinah Louise Lynch Taylor as much as I enjoy those with Taylor himself. The president often refers to her as "his source of strength . . . his inspiration."[34] In a telephone conversation, Dinah told me about meeting, marrying and sharing life with Jim Taylor.

The two met when Dinah, after her junior year at UK, moved to Williamsburg to help her sister with childcare and take summer classes in chemistry that were prerequisites to dietetics courses she would have to take at UK her senior year. Shortly after her arrival in Williamsburg, her sister took her to the Wigwam, a popular hangout for the College students. There she saw Taylor, the only student in the room dressed in a suit and tie, carrying a briefcase; she was not impressed. Shortly afterward, Taylor saw her in the library and asked her for a date. He must have been very impressive on that date; two weeks later they were engaged to be married.

Dinah finished her degree at UK the following year and the two married on May 24, 1968. Taylor graduated on May 25, with a contract to start working at Cumberland on May 27. The two moved into a trailer near the campus, and Dinah worked in social work for public assistance and later for mental health. In July of 1972, when their son was born, the two agreed that Dinah should quit her work outside the home. Taylor continued working at Cumberland until moving to Scarritt College, a move that lasted only eight months before his return to the campus at Williamsburg.

When asked how she felt when Taylor was named president, Dinah said she was very pleased for him. He had told her about his first view of the campus: he had gotten off the bus from Michigan at a wrong stop and had to walk across the bridge and through the town of Williamsburg to reach the campus property. As he stood on the bridge and looked at the campus on the hill, he had thought to himself, "One day I'll be president here." She knew that he had worked hard as a student and in various positions he had held on the campus, and she did not believe anyone could work harder or care more about the institution.

Dinah's first disappointment as first lady of the campus came when Mrs. Boswell invited her to see the president's house for the first time. She was horrified by how dilapidated it was and returned to the house where she and Taylor were living to announce that they should continue to live there, not in the designated president's house. However, after she invited a few of the wives of the trustees to see what had been the home of the Boswells, they convinced their husbands that one of the first priorities under Taylor should be the renovation of that house. The degree she completed at UK in Vocational Home Economics (which, at that time, generally led to employment as a public school teacher) has served Dinah well as she has worked on that house and helped with the design for other properties. Her education and natural talents also help as she hosts frequent social events.

She was, she admits, a little concerned about her responsibility for overseeing the renovation of her new home because the house had always been viewed as the special project of the daughter of one of the men who had helped establish the College; apparently not even a chair was moved from its original place in the house without that woman's permission. Over the course of the year Dinah was overseeing the changes at the house, she heard rumors that the woman was complaining about how Dinah was modernizing a house that should have been preserved in its original condition. Although she did bring modern conveniences to the house, Dinah made the architecture and décor representative of the style popular when it was built. When she invited the person whom she expected to be very critical of the changes to see the renovated house, the woman was so impressed she ordered the same curtains Dinah had installed.

Taylor had other things occupying his mind and was not involved in the renovation, so he did not see the house until the renovations were completed. When he saw the finished work, he was pleased, and he knew he could never have made the house as attractive and accommodating as his wife had. Their son, Dinah admits, found the house a great place to play, and the house seemed to welcome him. Young Jim was the first child to live there; the other occupants had all been childless or had grown children by the time they moved into the house.

Planning and serving as hostess for special events comes naturally to Dinah. She has, over the more than 33 years Taylor has been president, held hundreds of dinners, parties and receptions. One of her favorites is dinners for the trustees; she has developed a unique theme for each. Taylor's favorite seems to be the one she planned for his sixty-fifth birthday: when a large cake was wheeled into the dining room after dinner and everyone began to sing "Happy Birthday," she jumped out of the cake to add the final "Happy birthday, Mr. President," dressed as an aging Marilyn Monroe.

One advice Dinah gives to wives of new college presidents is to "be your own self; don't try to be what the former president's wife was." Mrs. Boswell had taught French at the College but seldom accompanied her husband on fund-raising trips or to campus events. Dinah never taught, but she has logged many miles as a travel companion for her husband, and she frequently attends events on the campus.

Another piece of advice is related to an event she held for a major donor; she arranged a very elaborate dinner, complete with lots of silver and fine china. When she began to worry that the guest of honor was not present, she asked one of those who was related to him when she should expect him to appear. The response was, "Why, Mrs. Taylor, he's dead." She then asked when his wife would arrive; she received the same response, "Why Mrs. Taylor, she's dead also." Dinah's advice is always be certain the guest for whom you reserve a chair is still living. In her words: "It is a good idea for spouses to understand totally what is going on before they attend any event." She reminds new first ladies to "always be yourself and always pace yourself; remember that what you do once, you will be expected to do forever."

Being a mother to Young Jim and getting her master's degree at Cumberland in early childhood education helped her in another of the roles she assumed as the wife of the president: she became, in her words, "a mother to the students," learning their names (a feat several mentioned), attending events for them and generally helping them feel at home on the campus.[35] When Art Levine wrote the story of his presidency at Bradford College for my first book about colleges that had closed or reinvented themselves, he said that when a student couple broke up at the college, he knew about it.[36] Cumberland College has always had that kind of feel—a place where people know and care when others are distressed.

Dinah often represents Taylor at campus events when he is not available, and she travels with him to visit donors and potential donors so often that her son, who must have had many babysitters on which to base this opinion, once told his Sunday School teacher that "parents make the best babysitters." Dinah even has what her husband calls "her own development program," sending cards to donors to remind them that their contributions are appreciated.

Perhaps the program most special to her is the one she developed after the most tragic event in her and Taylor's lives: Young Jim was killed on the eve of his high school graduation in 1991. He was on his way to visit a cousin who had just faced a personal tragedy when his car ran off the wet highway. Dinah was struck, after the difficult days of the funeral and almost unbearable grief, by how no one seemed to want to face her and Jim when they most needed people to reflect their care and concern. So when she read in the local paper about parents who had lost children, she started contacting them, letting them know that she understood their grief and was there if they needed her. She contacted a couple who had lost two sons, and they called and wanted to talk with her because they wanted to meet someone who had survived a similar tragedy. As she received notes from various parents talking about their children, she understood that their stories needed be preserved and shared. She suggested the parents should find a symbol that represented their sons or daughters and tell others to remember their children when they saw that symbol. The symbol she selected for Young Jim was the Pegasus; he had loved horses, and now, Dinah believes, he has wings himself.

With Young Jim's life insurance, Dinah started a newsletter inviting other parents of children who had died to create a symbol and share their stories about their children. In a few short years, she was sending out hundreds of these newsletters, doing all the labor herself. Later she developed a website which has roughly 3000 families listed who can stay in touch with each other and can be contacted by others facing similar grief and despair, and Dinah would send a card on each child's birth and death dates. Typically she sent about 200 cards each month. She kept up this mission for over 18 years, but when she was diagnosed with severe fibromyalgia and on the advice of physicians, she stopped trying to maintain the newsletter and stopped sending the cards, though the website is still in operation. A book has been written by the woman whom Dinah first contacted to start her efforts to help parents dealing with the loss of a child—*Children of the Dome*—a reference to the painting of some of the lost children and their symbols in the dome of the Cumberland Inn.[37]

Dinah has remained her own self, driven by her personal goals and limitations, but she has served, as Taylor has, as a guiding light for the College and those associated with it. Faculty frequently mention Dinah's devotion to the College when someone mentions her husband's dedicated service. She has made the same commitments as her husband and has devoted her life to serving others just as he has.

Cabinet

In the final decades of the twentieth century, complaints about higher education grew: "overpriced and poor-quality products, poor service and inattention to customers, inefficient and bureaucratic, unwilling to adapt to new markets, technologically backward, administratively bloated, more concerned with frills rather than the core product."[38] Institutions of higher education were repeatedly characterized as being poorly managed. Historians criticized one major university for both its record keeping and its practices related to finances: ". . . Its financial records seemed to be maintained in pen and ink in schoolboy notebooks. The cautious thrift of the place was well revealed by its maintaining balances of several million dollars in non-interest gathering checking accounts, with the business manager pleased that the bank did not charge for checks written."[39] Contrary to such criticisms, the administrative practices at UC seem solid. President Taylor has been able to find administrators as dedicated to the institution as he is and as competent in their roles as he is in his—and he has worked to keep them because he knows that beyond having the ability to raise money and the power to decide how money is spent, a president's other major source of influence is choosing the right people to do what he thinks needs to be done. Frequently, Taylor says, **"The job of the chief administrators is to bring the university in line with what the president is out there telling people it is."**

Until 1920, the president often served as the sole administrator, overseeing the work of a college—fund-raising, hiring/firing faculty, recruiting students, and often even teaching a class or two and coaching athletic teams. In 1920 the first academic dean at the institution, Arkley Wright, was named; he served six years. Wright was followed by Parry Jones, who served 34 years under two presidents. In 1961 Elmer Charles Masden became academic dean and served 19 years under President Boswell. When Boswell retired, Masden left the dean's office. Early, then a faculty member in math, became the Vice President for Academic Affairs and served from 1981 until 2002, when poor health forced his retirement. Other administrative offices have been established over the years, and those holding the various positions of leadership in those offices have tended to be fiercely loyal to the institution and its president. Many of those in office have graduated from the Cumberland and have remained on the campus for long periods of time. When the 2002 retirement of Early was announced, the top five administrators then at the College had a total of 155 combined years of service there, and four of the five were graduates of the College. Those five were Taylor, class of 1968; Colegrove, Vice President for Student Services, class of 1971 and at the College from 1973-1987 and 1989 until current date; Early, class of 1959 and at the College from 1969 until 2002; Ramey, in charge of business operations from 1968 until 2003; and Sue Wake, Vice President for Institutional Advancement, class of 1970 and employed at Cumberland from 1970 until the current date.[40] These people apparently feel as many I met who are employed by the College: they cannot imagine being anywhere else.

Taylor's translation of the Peter Drucker statement that "Management is doing things right; leadership is doing the right things"[41] is **"Presidents should make sure the right things are done while vice presidents should ensure things are done right."** While it is the president's responsibility to create the systems within which managers can manage and to change these systems when necessary to grow, take advantage of opportunities or avoid problems, it is the managers' responsibilities to operate those systems of people and facilities to assure the institution runs efficiently and effectively every hour of every day.[42] It is the fortunate institution that has both good leadership and good management. Although the major administrators at UC all work hard to fulfill the goal of making sure that the right things are done right, they all agree that none of the administrators can match Taylor's energy or ability to focus.

Having served as the chief academic officer under Taylor for 21 years, Early has some great insights about what it can be like to work for him. One frustration he learned to endure was Taylor's tendency to generate lots of ideas. Early often joked, "President Taylor has a hundred new ideas a month and it is my job to stomp out ninety-nine of them." When Early found the ideas related to academic programs inappropriate, he could not simply tell Taylor that the idea was not workable; he had to generate data that would support his position. When health matters forced Early's retirement and Good was named his replacement, Early gave Good a file that contained Taylor's ideas and Early's data related to them that had been gathered over 21 years. He prepared Good to see those ideas appear again over the next several years; he did not prepare him for what happened: Good saw most of those ideas over the next six months.[43]

Joe Stepp remembers that when he became the president at Alice Lloyd, Taylor "took him under his wing." Since he especially admires Taylor's ability to find and keep good administrators, he once asked Taylor what he looked for when hiring a vice president; Taylor took the time to write his response: **"When looking for a person to fill a major administrative position, I look for someone who is highly intelligent, loyal to both the institution and me—someone I can empower to do a job and support in their decision making."**[44] And what Early and others seem to appreciate most about working for Taylor is that "he believes in getting people that he trusts around him and he lets them do what he thinks that they ought to be doing."[45] The advice he often gives new presidents such as Stepp is similar to that he gives to those who help him carry out his major administrative responsibilities:

> **. . . Don't strive for recognition or appreciation; rather try to please the man or woman in the mirror and the God you serve, because . . . to please one person is too often to displease another. Don't misspend emotional energy on why alumni don't do more, or why the community doesn't appreciate the institution—all are counterproductive.**

> **. . . Always do what is in the best interest of the institution without giving sway to presidential whims or thoughts of legacy.**[46]

Obviously, responsibilities and the qualities needed to fulfill them vary according to the position held, but a general description of the responsibilities of the members of the cabinet could be to help set the vision and course of action for the College and to lead the way in fulfilling that vision. In the area of academic affairs, fulfilling the vision meant, as Early said, "building a faculty and enabling the faculty to do their job better."[47] Good reports that in his years at UC, his major focus was on the faculty and the more traditional liberal arts curriculum, while Taylor's was toward a more utilitarian curriculum focusing primarily on the professions, and a lot of time was spent reconciling the different positions. Good, now an Associate Professor in Educational Leadership and Policy Analysis at a major public university, says that he has come to appreciate how much more quickly change can be implemented in a culture like that at UC than it can be in a state university system, and he misses at least one aspect of the culture at UC: it was easy to know what was happening across the campus at least most of the time. Good, like a number of other administrators (and faculty) who have left a small private college for a large state one, has come to see how green the grass at the small college can be.[48]

A *Chronicle* blog lists the attributes major administrators (deans/vice-presidents) should have: inclusiveness (willingness to listen to everyone); delegation; sincerity, decisiveness (once everyone has had a say, the administrator makes a decision); accountability; optimism; realism; frankness; self-effacement (humility); collegiality; honesty; trustworthiness (does what he or she promises or explains why he or she could not); and morality (can be counted on to do what he or she believes is right for all those concerned). As one respondent indicates, a successful institutional leader must be "fully immersed in the position." *The Chronicle* comment concludes, faculty members "don't particularly like being told what to do" but "they abhor a leadership vacuum."[49]

The current Vice President for Academic Affairs, Larry Cockrum, seems to fulfill the need of the faculty for a "sounding board." Faculty with whom I met spoke highly about how comfortable they are with Cockrum, even though they readily admit that his focus is on building the skills of the students while theirs may remain on helping the students consider issues related to living a life of meaning as well as helping them develop skills leading to employment in specific fields. While they do not think that Cockrum welcomes long theoretical discussions and that his mind is more that of a business executive than that of a philosopher, they do believe they can say anything to him and know that he always keeps their best interest at the forefront of the institutional agenda.

The cabinet meets weekly and each representative reports on the issues and progress in his or her division. What those who have served as members of the president's cabinet have learned is that Taylor "is difficult to work for if you are not as dedicated to the college as he is . . . . his intensity is like a fire. If you stand close and you see your role just as a job, you are going to get burned."[50] In knowing that about the president, those who have served for so many years as central administrators at UC are clearly as dedicated to the institution as he is. Taylor often reflects on his appreciation of the value of a strong staff: **"I've had people surrounding me on whose shoulders I stand who work beyond the call of duty and who believe in our mission passionately. This is key."**[51]

Governance

Over the years I have heard complaints by faculty and staff at multiple colleges that their college does not have a way for faculty to provide input into institutional decisions. This concern is one that appeared frequently in my interviews for books I wrote about closed or reinvented colleges. It appears that President Taylor agrees with Stuart Kirk, a recent president at the College of Santa Fe. When Kirk's faculty asked if he believed in shared governance, his response was that his idea of shared governance is that faculty govern the curriculum and their classrooms and the president and trustees govern the business of the college.[52] Even Bowen, President Emeritus of Princeton and of the Andrew W. Mellon Foundation, in talking about the role of faculty in governing and administering a college, reminds readers: "There is a delicate balance to be struck between keeping an institution moving forward and reining in expectations that have no chance of being satisfied."[53] The down-sized economy has, according to Taylor, united the staff and faculty in some ways; everyone feels a stronger than usual obligation to work together to overcome the problems created by the loss of income from the endowment and the decline in giving between 2008 and 2011.[54]

Since salaries contribute roughly 70 percent of most budgets, faculty and staff need to be kept informed about the various priorities for operating the institution to help them understand the limits of what is realistic for the institution in terms of benefits and salaries, and they may need to be reminded that trustees are often forced by the demands of external pressures to make decisions quickly; trustees seldom have the luxury of the classroom where issues can be debated and analyzed in great detail over long periods of time.

Faculty need to have a voice early in a decision-making process even as they understand that final decisions are made by major administrators and trustees, but having a voice does not necessarily require or mean having consensus. James L. Fisher, former president of Towson State and author of numerous works on leadership in higher education, encourages presidents to make decisions without worrying about taking the time necessary to build consensus.[55] And generally that is a practice Taylor follows. When major budget cuts were necessary in 2008-2009 and the following few years, in explaining to his board the decisions he and his cabinet had made, Taylor also described why he did not involve the faculty in this instance: time was of the essence and "most faculty are likely to slow change down, to criticize issues, to ponder questions philosophically, and to join in endless analysis and endless conversations . . . ." Then he congratulated his faculty for their ability to adapt to the changing environment: "Fortunately, our faculty has been a team player in adapting to the changing environment."[56] **Taylor's philosophy is not to focus on "solving problems" so much as on "seizing opportunities,"** and such "seizing" often requires quick action.

When I was a graduate intern at the Council of Higher Education for the state of Kentucky, the head of that office, Harry Snyder, was once asked if politics were involved in the decisions made by the organization. His response was that there were indeed politics involved in the decision-making process of the Council, but the politics at the Council were never as brutal as those on the college campuses. Taylor seems to agree that **the college campus is "a community in conflict . . . . There are abrasive** and adversarial relationships and power plays, and vested interests [on college campuses], but we must make something good out of it all. A president must make something positive happen in the midst of such constraints."[57] Fortunately for presidents and trustees in Kentucky, the state is an employment-at-will state; thus, the employer or employee can end a working relationship at any time for any reason without notice— unless the reason for the termination is protected by federal legislation (age, sex, religion, etc.). When I was president of the ACA and Taylor was chair of the board, he encouraged me to take comfort in that fact when evaluating employees, but to always treat others with respect and fairness; in his word, ". . . **People are more important than programs or projects.**"

As Taylor said in his speech to the National Society of Fund Raising Executives in 1987: **"A college president has many roles and has been called many things—planner and manager, lobbyist and politician, myth maker and myth breaker, leader and follower, mediator and negotiator, apologist and advocate, and a host of other names, some of which are unspeakable."** At one time or another, a president must be all of these for the variety of his constituencies. Taylor refuses to allow anyone under his authority to be apathetic or impatient, to settle for mediocrity or to reflect insecurities. While he holds each employee accountable for success in the relevant divisions, he holds no one more accountable and expects no one to accomplish more than he expects himself to be accountable and to achieve.

Taylor knows that even with a staff of competent people, one of his responsibilities is to keep them all motivated: in his words, **"A president must be a perpetual optimist, rallying the troops around a shared vision and sense of purpose. All hands on deck, all rowing in the same direction."**[58] Taylor admits that giving faculty and staff a sense of ownership of a project may require offering a deliberately imperfect compromise, but Taylor welcomes "lofty goals bubbling up from the faculty, trustees and [other] constituencies through strategic planning." He knows that **change comes best when goals are approached "in incremental steps with a series of small wins leading to a tipping point."**[59] But when the score remains tied or close to a tie, the final move at UC is determined by Taylor. As President Stepp described him, Taylor is "a coach for the faculty and staff—a coach who knows the plays his team needs to run."

CHAPTER 3: FUNDING

The most critical responsibility of the president is "to provide the financial resources necessary to carry on the enterprise through raising money and through tight-fisted fiscal management of institutional assets . . . . A dream without funding is an hallucination."[1] In a 2013 survey of almost 400 college presidents, the two items accounting for over half the time on the presidents' daily schedules were fund-raising and managing budgets.[2]

Raising Money

No matter how strong the leadership of a college might be, without adequate financial backing, it is hard for an institution to thrive. Often trustees are not fully aware of the seriousness of the financial stress under which the college operates and some presidents accept their role without fully realizing the responsibilities they will have for building its financial stability. Having served multiple roles at Cumberland College, Taylor became president fully aware of the financial challenges, the major one for Cumberland being the need to sustain a strong scholarship program. After a few years in the office, he concluded **". . . The determining factor in the future of private colleges and universities will not be the high tuition cost, but the availability of student aid funds . . . . The important thing to a student is not the tuition charge made by the institution, but the money that is required out of his or her own pocket. This means that we must focus our attention as never before on student aid endowment funds and scholarships."**[3] Raising the money to support the students and build the University has been Taylor's major focus throughout his career.

President Taylor's approach to fund-raising has become legendary; his persistence is heroic. I used to hear stories about Taylor's visits to New York—where he would walk into a major bank and ask to see the president. When the receptionist would say that the bank president was busy—or out, Taylor would state simply that he would wait—and wait he did, sometimes for a day or more, to see the person with the potential of making a significant contribution to the College.

When other college presidents seek out his advice, it is usually advice related to fund-raising they want. In the last twenty years he has raised roughly $10-$15 million every year except in the years between 2008 and 2011 when the national economic picture was extremely dire, and he warns others never to succumb to the tendency to blame economic recessions or the growing competition in the fund-raising arena from public institutions for any decline in contributions. He does not believe that people give just because they have money. And he encourages a team approach to fund-raising. He recognizes that his success has been built, in part, on the work of the presidents who preceded him and on the staff who surround him.[4]

As was pointed out in the chapter on past presidents of the College, the first man to serve as president realized in less than a year that raising money was a full-time job, especially since the students attending were not able to contribute much in tuition toward the cost of their education. At that time the institution consisted of the president and faculty. There were no deans or vice-presidents to whom President Johnson could delegate responsibilities. In addition to serving as the leader of the College, Johnson was also pastor. At 27 years of age, Johnson gave up the presidency to spend his time raising money for the College. One of the windows in the chapel on the campus includes a picture of Johnson riding a horse with his hand out—as he often did throughout the region, accepting pennies and farm animals as gifts. But it was not only the small contributions that residents and churches of Kentucky could give to Johnson that sustained the College and allowed it to grow; it was the contributions of people like John D. Rockefeller and Andrew Carnegie, with their gifts of $4,500 and $18,000 respectively, that helped assure the continuation of the College in its early years. And Johnson was often required to raise matching funds for those from the large donors. He was always successful in fulfilling the commitments to raise the funds needed, but the work required long hours of travel and meetings, often in bad weather on horseback through rough terrains. For example, 93 donors contributed to the match required for the Rockefeller gift; some contributions were for one dollar. He died at age 30 of tuberculosis, but he left an example of persistence and diligence that others would follow in building the College.[5]

Later, major foundations—such as the Pew Trusts, James Graham Brown, Andrew W. Mellon, Williams Randolph Hearst—helped fuel the passion that drove the College, but as the numbers of colleges increased and even those started by state governments began to appeal to the foundation world for financial support, it became increasingly difficult for a small college to compete for the dollars available. The presidents, especially those of the small rural colleges located far away from the headquarters of corporations that might give in their local communities, had to be increasingly creative to find the funding for the new facilities and programs that a changing world demanded.

The fact that before Taylor was president he was in charge of fund-raising for the College prepared him for what would become his major responsibility. During those early years in his presidency, Taylor was able to generate gifts from numerous foundations, including Jessie Smith Noyes, James

Graham Brown, Kresge, Max C. Fleishman, Dewitt Wallace, and Arthur Vining Davis. In the 1970s, such gifts were critical to the strong growth of the College, and at that time Taylor was basically a "one-man show," depending for assistance on President Boswell in soliciting funds. Then in 1979 he submitted a proposal to Boswell to restructure the development office and declared, "This proposal in all probability has to do with the eventual life and death of the college" as well as with "the improvement of efficiency and productivity." He focused in part on the fact that many of the sources of support on which the College had depended could not provide the financial resources that would keep pace with increasing costs and growing expectations.[6] Compared to most of the other private colleges in Kentucky in the 1970s, Cumberland College fared well in the fund-raising arena—but the institution still often faced annual operating deficits.

With the acceptance of Taylor's proposal, public relations, alumni affairs and fund-raising were centralized. The College focused on answering a critical question as the first step in developing a fund-raising strategy: "What is it we do different from, other than, better than, or . . . uniquely alone?" Taylor and his administrative staff have always been aware of the fact that it would be a mistake to try to make the College like one of the elite private colleges, in part because donors interested in providing resources to such institutions are probably already giving to one. What Cumberland needs to show potential donors is not how Cumberland can imitate wealthy, highly selective institutions, but how and what the College contributes to a population different from those at the elites. **"It does not want to become what it is not, but the college does want to become more than it is."**[7]

Under Taylor's proposal, a weekly meeting was instituted to reflect on the work of the previous week and plan for the current one; goals were set for the work of the alumni director (including expectations for the number of contributions made by alumni and names of potential donors), and for the public relations officer (who could also be expected to serve in the area of deferred giving). Finally the development staff was to be increased to include at least two field staff and a grant writer/research specialist to assist those working in the field.

Today, in the basement of one of the major buildings on campus is an office staffed with six professionals (each of whom has been with the College for at least 30 years) and two work-study students. Serving across the country are three full-time and three part-time field staff assigned by geographical areas to cultivate foundations, corporations and other prospects. Kay Manning oversees the office staff responsibilities, including identifying potential donors, soliciting them with letters prepared by the president, and maintaining contact to thank them after they have given.

This operation has grown from the one established by Taylor prior to his leaving the office of development to become president in 1980. At that time, every letter, every envelope and every file was prepared and maintained by hand. While a lot of the data is now on computers, there are still rows of file cabinets containing hard copies of correspondence to donors. The office maintains a file on every document mailed to donors or potential donors, the numbers mailed, and the visits made.

Field staff responsibilities include travel to assigned geographic areas to cultivate donors or potential donors. It is their reports on the contacts made that guide the proposal writing staff in preparation of proposals for funding; field staff call on donors to recognize gifts received as well as to encourage future contributions. They are also expected to communicate with donors and alumni frequently by phone, to establish advisory committees in communities where the potential for identifying new contributors is strong, and to make visits to current and prospective donors as needed.[8] Like so many UC employees, Manning has been at the University for many years and knows the processes she oversees so well that maintaining operations in her office seems simple when she describes it, but to an outsider, the office may seem overwhelmingly complicated.

Much of the success of the fund-raising program at UC can be summed up in two words: targeting and tracking. The office staff identify potential donors and the field staff track the personal contacts made. Taylor talks about **institutional advancement or development as a matrix: under targeting would be psychographics—the psychological profile of the potential donor that would lead to his/her giving; and demographics— the personal characteristics of the potential donor. Under tracking**

would be recency—how recently has a donor given; amount—how much has he/she given; and frequency—how often has he/she given.[9]

It should come as no surprise that the more people college representatives see, the more requests they make, the more proposals they submit, the more money they are likely to bring to a college. Taylor believes that personal solicitation is the major avenue to raising gifts, and he has never underestimated the importance of face-to-face visits. Years ago, Robert Zemsky, well known for his work in higher education at the University of Pennsylvania and the numerous books he has published on the topic, said in a conference call with a number of the ACA administrators that major requests should be made, if not face-to-face, at least voice-to-voice. An illustration of this principal is that involving a proposal of matrimony; few are naïve enough to expect the same response to such a proposal if it is made in writing or by phone instead of in person. Taylor's comment that reflects the importance of close contact with constituents came in a speech he wrote in 2007 for a Council of Independent Colleges (CIC) meeting of presidents. Quoting former Louisiana Governor Edwin Edwards, he said, **"Never write in a letter what you can say over the phone; never say on the phone what you can whisper in the ear; never whisper in an ear when you can raise an eyebrow; never raise an eyebrow when a wink will do."**

All of those in the development office realize that since 80 to 90 percent of gift income comes from 5 to 10 percent of an institution's donors, that 5 to 10 percent should receive the bulk of their time and attention, but that time and attention does not generally take the form of developing color brochures. While employing virtually each new technological advance in soliciting donors, the staff are continuously reminded that the need of human beings to be wanted and recognized never changes. Despite the frequent training sessions for staff to keep them current in the field of unitrusts, annuity trusts, pooled income funds, charitable lead trusts, life tenancy agreements, gift annuities and other ways of making contributions, Taylor encourages simplicity in approaches to donors and potential donors. He suggests frequent follow-up to recognize contributions and inform donors about how their gifts have benefited the College. He wants the donors to gain from their gifts—to enjoy the satisfaction that comes from the knowledge that their gifts have made the world a better place.

Taylor cautions **not to approach fund raising as a desperate plea for help, but as a natural part of ensuring a solid base of financial stability for the college. He advises presidents to maximize their time on fund-raising by focusing on those who give or might give a substantial amount of funds and letting the field staff and mail and phone solicitation teams handle the others. Additional advice is to listen more than you talk; to keep the conversation focused on stories about people, not data or policies or procedures; to keep the imagination focused and exciting; to try to capture the interest and personal commitment, as well as funding; to try to make the donor's interest area match needs of the institution.**[10]

In my experiences in fund-raising with foundations, however, it was clear that in some cases the institution must focus on needs that reflect the interest areas of the funder. Simply put, the needs of the college and the interests of the donors should match for an investment in the college to be likely to reap the greatest benefits.

Obviously, UC solicits alumni from the time they graduate. Unfortunately, few are able to respond with contributions since over 60 percent of the graduates stay in the region and most, regardless of where they settle after graduation, enter fields where incomes are low. Also, since the College was a junior college for years up until 1961, those who completed their college educations at a four-year college are most likely to give, when they give, to the senior college. Still, alumni participation is a "wee bit" over the national average.[11]

Even nineteen years after becoming president Taylor was still focused on fund-raising, declaring, "**. . . I only masquerade as a college president since my first love is institutional advancement.**" At one point early in his tenure, he estimated that he spent at least 15 percent of his time in visits to potential and existing donors; later, he estimated he was spending 75 percent of his time fund-raising. In a recent year, he reflected on the 180 nights he had spent on the road in that year. While some of that time was spent conducting work on behalf of the University's general operations and performing services for the accrediting agencies and other organizations, most of those visits were to encourage contributions. Following is one story among the legends about Taylor's leadership that illustrates the stress so much travel can create: waking up in a hotel one morning, Taylor noticed on the mirror in the room a logo that said "Holiday Inn, Cincinnati, Ohio." He called his assistant and said, "Sue, I'm in Cincinnati." She said, "Yes, Sir." He said, "Why?"

When people have commented on how much time Taylor spends on the road, he usually responds, "**I have never found any friends or funds under my desk.**"[12] Still, there are stories about how Taylor is quick to know how to respond to questions when a potential donor calls him at his office. When a donor who had made her fortune with Harcourt Brace Jovanovich and had contributed significantly to Cumberland College died, the attorney involved in settling the estate, along with the presidents of Bryn Mawr, Mount Holyoke, Smith, Vassar, and Radcliff—all other colleges involved in her will—called President Taylor and asked, "How is it these presidents have never heard of Cumberland?" Taylor responded quickly: "Gee, that's funny. We've heard about each of them."[13] Cumberland received the gift designated without any further questions—or implications.

Every strategic plan for the institution makes clear the importance of raising the money to implement improvements and defines the specific improvements to be made or at least the specific areas in which improvements will be made. Over the years, the focus of such plans has moved from specific amounts to be raised for each project under consideration to the area of concern with funding mentioned for an area. For example, the plan developed in the early 1980s listed 10 specific projects, such as building a new residence hall, with figures ranging from $20 million to increase the endowment to $39,000 for equipment for the mining technology program.[14] By the early part of the twenty-first century, the strategic plan included more general priorities: Goal I was "Strengthen the University's academic program," and Goal II was "Strengthen the co-curricular facilities and programs necessary to support the needs and expectations of a diverse campus community."[15] By 2010, the plan reflected focus on recruitment and retention: improving the admissions process for undergraduates, graduates and professional students was the first priority and strengthening the academic programs was priority number two.[16] After a few years as president, Taylor knew the directions he wanted to take in the area of development; and, apparently, he felt it less important to list specific expenditures anticipated than areas where the College needed to invest.

Despite his concern that those who are the wealthiest in the nation—the 20 percent who earn more money than those in the other 80 percent collectively—are tending more and more to support only those organizations that directly benefit themselves, Taylor believes that there remain many people who, when they believe in an institution, will find a way to give even when the economy is weak—that people do not give money simply because it is plentiful. And those who have given that I have spoken with over the years appreciate the fact that when they give to UC, they are told specifically how their gift has and will benefit the institution and the region.

Once, I was sitting at a table with trustees and spouses of a college in the Northeast where I was serving on the board. In talking to another trustee across the table, I described the practice of having college representatives visit people who make contributions to the college. The spouse of a former trustee sitting next to me said, "I know that college; that's Cumberland College." I was surprised she recognized Cumberland with so little information about it. She continued with a complaint: "And I don't appreciate having strangers appear at my door unannounced." She described a visit she had from a Cumberland College representative at her home in Florida. She thanked the young man but asked him not to come unannounced again. I asked her if the representative had called and asked for a visit, would she have invited him to her house. She said she would not have. She continued to tell me that she was even more surprised by a visit the next year at her home in New Hampshire—where her mail is delivered to a post office box. When she asked the Cumberland College representative how he found her home address, he said that the local police had given it to him. I announced my assumption: "So you won't give money again to Cumberland." Her response was also a surprise. She said that of course she would give again; she very much appreciated learning how her gift had been useful." Taylor agrees with Father Theodore Hesburgh's 1980 comment about the importance of vision: **"The most important contribution a president can make to institutional advancement is to articulate a vision of the institution so persistently and persuasively that it becomes shared by all constituencies, internal and external, who adapt it as their own."**[17] It seems the advice about having a vision all can share was at work in this case of the donor who did not want her privacy disturbed but was clearly impressed with the information provided.

President Stepp points out that the major reason for Taylor's success in fund-raising is that his commitment to and passion for UC is obvious to those he is asking. I suggest his success is primarily due to his persistence and that of his staff.

(See Appendix C for gift income by year.)

Fiscal Oversight

President Taylor does realize that fund-raising is only part of the financial operations of a college. He warns, **"While fund-raising can enhance the long-term future of an institution, in the near term it cannot prop up an institution's budget. Expenditures must be controlled because if your out-go exceeds your income, then your upkeep will be your downfall."**[18]

When Taylor became president August 1,1980, the College had a reasonably strong budget, generated in large measure by the enrollments which had grown to about 2000. For twenty-five years after Taylor's inauguration, total enrollments remained fairly stable—varying between 1500 and about 2000 between the 1981-1982 year and the 2005-2006 year. But the annual unrestricted budgets moved steadily upward—from just over $7 million in 1981-1982 to over $25 million for 2005-2006. Tuition clearly did not account for the increase in income during those years; Taylor's expertise in the fund-raising arena accounted for most of the difference. In 1980-1981 gift income was about $2.6 million; in 2005-2006, it was $10,678,836. Just as enrollment varied in those 25 years, and the increase was not evenly distributed, so the gift income went up and down, but in the years prior to 2008, it was generally about $10 million, reaching almost $15 million one year. And for that reason and because the College has kept a tight rein on expenditures, Taylor could report to SACS during a 1995 visit: ". . . We have never shown a deficit in the current fund." After giving dropped over $6 million in 2008, the University established a $5 million line of credit for short term financing but has never used more than $2 million of it. Ever the optimist, Taylor reports that when a trustee asked him why the gift income for 2008 was down by over $6 million, he said, "How fortunate we were to be down by only $6,614,370 in this climate."[19]

In a discussion with his board, Taylor explained the rationale for using money to market the institution and recruit students instead of adding that amount of money to the endowment. As he explained: **"A mere 100 additional students is worth over $700,000 a year to us . . . . If you think it is better to have a million drawing nine percent or $90,000 a year than to spend a million to help recruit and retain 100 more students resulting in $700,000 a year, then your math is different from mine."**[20] He frequently stresses to faculty and staff the importance of saving money by carefully using every resource so the University can best serve the students of the region. But major expenditures include not just attracting students, but also providing scholarship money that most of the applicants need each year and providing the learning experiences that justify the expenditures.

With the 2005-2006 year, enrollment began to grow significantly (in large measure due to the increase in numbers of graduate and online courses), increasing to 3,785 total students (3,254 FTE) by 2011-2012.[21] But although the total of annual contributions for several years after 2005 grew to almost $15 million in 2006-2007 and just under $13 million the next year, in 2008 contributions fell significantly. They have stayed under the $10 million mark from that time until the current fiscal year (2012-2013). The market collapse created financial hardships for the University, cutting deeply into the endowment. Even though increases in enrollment helped offset those loses, the University was still forced to take steps to reduce the budget by roughly $500,000 per year.

In the book about *Nine University Presidents Who Saved Their Institutions,* organizational development and cost reductions were mentioned as a solution to a financial crisis many more times than revenue enhancement, enrollment management or gift solicitation. Many presidents, it seems, have more faith in balancing a budget through careful fiscal management than through raising increasing amounts of money. One president, in explaining how he saved a nearly closed college explained: ". . . I focused much more on expense than on revenue," on "strict expense management, growth by substitution, cost control."[22]

During cost-cutting measures at UC, faculty and staff positions have been eliminated. At the opening of the 2009 school year, Taylor announced to faculty and staff that as the result of the national economic conditions, he would have to freeze salaries; focus on recruiting and retaining more students; raise more money from private donors; and examine "each department in terms of size, cost, production of graduates, and centrality to institutional mission." Such review of programs in terms of cost related to productivity (i.e., numbers of majors) has resulted over the years in the closing of several departments, including philosophy and nursing. In describing the years following the 2008 market collapse, Taylor started a letter to the board in March of 2010: "I must confess the past 18 months have presented formidable challenges." And challenges have continued to plague all of higher education.

Among Taylor's greatest talents is the ability to make financial projections and adjust the work of the University to accommodate them. While the College has been able at various times of financial stress to hold normal expenditures steady or decrease them, investment has continued in what seems to promise to benefit the College's future growth—including online courses and new professional and graduate programs. As giving has declined, the College has offered an increasing array of professional and graduate programs that have attracted an increasing number of students, and (in most cases) graduate students pay the full tuition so discounting is not the issue it can be for undergraduate enrollments.

As a part of the "tight-fisted fiscal management of institutional assets," the investment policy of the institution is to hold 60 percent of the endowment in variable securities and 40 percent in fixed investments, but the investment officers have the discretion to vary as much as 20 percent in either direction: the ratio could be 80 percent and 20 percent.[23] The withdrawal policy is to take 5 percent of a three-year rolling average.[24] A professional investment company reports monthly to the board and provides suggestions on fund managers for consideration by the trustees.

In order to recruit quality students and retain them and to attract donors, the University has, on some occasions, used money in quasi-endowment to invest in capital improvements. In recent years, Taylor has explained to SACS that while the institution does carry debt, it is a small percentage of the net worth of the institution and compares favorably with the debt to asset ratio of other small private colleges in the region.[25] The trustees and president continue to try to have money in hand for new projects or at least to know from where the money is coming before a project is started.

Periodically, Taylor has to make tough decisions related to stabilizing the budget. One decision was to close the college's nursing program when there was a lot of pressure to continue it. A financial analysis indicated that the current program was losing money, and there was no way to change the program to recover the lost funds and create a financially sustainable one. Despite pressure from both inside and outside the college, the board agreed to discontinue the program through a teach-out that would allow existing students to complete their degrees. Faculty contracts were honored and students were given money to complete their degrees at Eastern Kentucky University, about an hour north of Cumberland College; travel expenses to and from Eastern were also covered for those who needed transportation. The decision saved over a million dollars in the first two years after implementation.[26]

Another decision related to stabilizing the budget as well as to updating the curriculum was a faculty buy-out plan rewarding long time faculty for their service and opening slots to employ new faculty with the credentials and training in new pedagogies to implement new courses and programs. For roughly 20 years, the College allowed faculty to retire early with special benefits that rewarded them for their many years of service. When accounting requirements changed and forced the anticipation of the retirement of faculty over a certain age and the listing of any amount they would receive under this early retirement plan as a liability, the benefit was suspended. During the 20 years the plan was an option, the College was well served by it. In one year, 17 faculty took early retirement and 15 new faculty were hired.[27]

(Appendix D reports on the unrestricted budget, expenditures and total revenue.)

CHAPTER 4: CULTURE

The culture of an institution is the beliefs, customs, and practices that identify the place. The culture of UC is defined by its mission, its people, and its activities. At Cumberland, the mission is to provide a liberal arts education enhanced by Christian values and a commitment to work and service. Faculty and staff, as well as the president and trustees, reflect genuine concern for those affiliated with the University and for the broader community. As the curriculum is revised and new courses and degrees are developed, faculty and staff explore new ways of teaching, assessing learning, and providing opportunities for service. The campus is made more attractive each year and people feel comfortable and safe on it. Multiple extracurricular experiences are provided to keep students active and involved in campus life, and the culture is enriched by visiting scholars and special performances. In summary, the culture of UC reflects many of the values of Appalachia at the same time that it exposes students to the beliefs, values, and practices of regions across the world.

Mission

Some colleges that have made significant changes in recruiting and funding priorities continue to claim missions that established the institutions, but it is clear from their actions that they are no longer committed to those original missions. The 1892-1893 catalog of the Williamsburg Institute reflects the mission to which it has held tightly: "It is the purpose of Williamsburg Institute to furnish thorough instruction and to give an opportunity for a first-class education at rates that are compatible with the means of mountain people."[1] Enrollment and financial aid and other data indicate no deviation from this mission.

The mission of the institution that became Cumberland College was typical of many colleges in the late 1800s that churches established to serve the citizens of the colonies. Ironically, what made Cumberland typical when it was established seems to be making it unique today. According to Heilman, in his explanation about why Cumberland is successful, "As many Christian colleges have waivered, moving farther and farther away from conservative philosophies, Cumberland's position in the world of higher education has become increasingly unique." Becoming unique is serving the institution well. Again, according to Heilman, "There are a lot of people who want to support institutions promoting conservatism and increasingly fewer such colleges for them to support."

These two facts—the institution has held fast to its original mission and that mission is more unique today than in the past—have contributed to its success. After listing Taylor's leadership as the major reason UC has been successful, Wheelan listed a second reason: "The university has a clear identity—everyone knows what it stands for . . . [and] the university has made programmatic changes to accommodate the realities of a sharply changing world—but it didn't change its core values." When Taylor talks about being true to himself, according to Heilman, he means "being true to the mission of the college": serving the poorest among us. Holding true to Christian principles in educating the poor has kept UC among the leading institutions in the Council for Christian Colleges and Universities (CCCU), an organization of over 100 colleges and universities. Remaining true to the values of the past while incorporating new approaches to pedagogy and new technologies into the courses taught on campus and online has given UC a unique position among many of the roughly 1600 private nonprofit colleges listed by the National Association of Independent Colleges and Universities (NAICU).

George Dehne of Dehne & Associates, a consulting firm specializing in marketing and strategic planning, has visited the campus on several occasions; he compares the missions of Berea College and Cumberland College: the two colleges have "driven the same message across the nation—there are a lot of poor kids who have great potential but need a college education they cannot afford to be able to realize their potential." Given the poverty in Appalachia, providing "a first-class education" at a cost the residents of the region can afford has been a constant challenge for the leaders of UC. Even today a large percent of the total budget of the University is devoted to providing scholarships that make it possible for the students to attend, 45 percent of whom come from the region. Despite the strong fund-raising record, having to devote so much of the annual budget to scholarships handicaps the institution in addressing other needs. Still, since the 1800s the College has made its major priority honoring the intent of those who originally founded it by providing quality educational experiences at minimal cost.

The history of the College published during its centennial celebration lists the Purposes and Objectives:

> Cumberland, "the College of the Kentucky Mountains," was founded in 1889 to provide indigenous leadership for the southern Appalachian region, based upon a quality educational program sustained by Christian values. To accomplish this purpose the College has the following specific objectives:
>
> 1. Cumberland seeks to perpetuate, by word and deed, those values which are derived from the Christian faith and thereby encourage students to develop a sense of self-worth and to establish patterns of personal integrity, self-discipline and social responsibility.
>
> 2. Cumberland seeks to equip each student with a liberal education which will encourage the student to think critically, appreciate broadly, and act intelligently and unselfishly.
>
> 3. Cumberland seeks to assist each student in understanding the cultural traditions of which each is a part.
>
> 4. Cumberland seeks to teach each student the importance of physical and mental well-being and how each may be maintained.
>
> 5. Cumberland seeks to provide academic specialization, insofar as it is possible within the broad framework of a liberal arts education, in order to develop each individual for effective leadership in his chosen profession, in the church of his choice, and in the geographical area where he will serve.

> With respect to the members of the faculty and administrative
> staff, our purpose is to maintain a sense of community which
> maximizes acceptance, mutual respect and individual worth;
> to serve as models of ideal persons and professions;
> and to pursue the most effective means of teaching and learning
> for the benefit of the entire academic community.
>
> With respect to the larger community, our purpose is to offer
> educational opportunities to students, regardless of race, religion,
> age, or financial status.[2]

When Taylor became president, he had long been committed to what the institution represented. A part of honoring any mission can require taking a stand on issues where various populations hold differing views. Those at UC, a professed Baptist institution, have taken some stands that have been unpopular with certain constituencies. It has not, however, done as some institutions and tried to hide its unpopular beliefs. Certainly it has not, as some have, covered up major incidents that could reflect negatively on the institution.

In *Wikipedia*, there are few entries related to colleges or universities where the contributors felt it necessary to devote an entire section to "controversies." Even in the entry for Penn State, the child sex abuse scandal covered widely by national media in 2011 and 2012 is barely mentioned in a short paragraph under the history of the college. Yet for UC (and a few other colleges with strong ties to conservative religions) *Wikipedia* includes a specific section marked "controversies." In the case of Cumberland, the issue that has the broadest coverage in that part of its *Wikipedia* entry is related to the position taken on sexual activities.

The College has never made a secret of its strong commitment to the Baptist Church and the interpretation of the Bible that the Church has professed. That philosophy reflects the high standards of behavior expected of students while recognizing that these standards may not be ones practiced by society in general or other denominations in particular. C. Roland Christensen, a renowned Harvard professor, has a philosophy that Cumberland College promotes: "I teach not only what I know, but what I am."[3]

This position was tested in the spring of 2006 when a sophomore theatre arts major discussed his "gay lifestyle" on a social networking site. The UC Student Handbook of 2005 indicates that a student can be expelled from the campus for engaging in pre-marital sex or promoting homosexuality: "Any students who engages in or promotes sexual behavior not consistent with Christian principles (including sex outside marriage and homosexuality) may be suspended or asked to withdraw from the University of the Cumberlands."

Throughout publicity surrounding the open discussions by the student of his sexual activities, representatives repeatedly explained that, from the perspective of the University, the issues were sex outside of marriage, the public display of a person's sexuality, and the obligation of the institution to enforce the rules prescribed for students. As the chair of the board commented when I spoke with him, enforcement of rules is critical and the only case he can remember where a student was expelled involved one who openly disobeyed rules governing student behavior. A student, whose name I have chosen to withhold, seems to have reflected the view of many when he wrote about his reactions to the case, "As a private institution, Cumberland has the right, and moral obligation, to set a standard for conduct."

Despite the continued focus by the media on the fact that the student who had violated the campus policy was gay and that efforts to penalize the University for discrimination were based on sexual orientation, the University did not waiver from its commitment to the sanctity of marriage as well as to that of marriage between male and female. Certainly when a student there commented to a reporter that she personally knew several dozen students on the campus who were gay, there was never any effort to identify those students and penalize them in any way;[4] they had never openly disobeyed student behavior policies. At an ACA meeting, I heard the vice president in the UC office of Academic Affairs at the time try to explain to a reporter that the violation of the code of behavior that was creating so much commotion was that of publicly displaying sexual behavior; the reporter's comment was, "There's no story in that." Thus the focus in the media remained on the fact that the student was homosexual. He transferred to a nearby public university for the following semester and never filed a grievance with any of the agencies that oversee such complaints of discrimination, but his disregard for the policies of the institution seems to have haunted the institution more than the individual. (See Appendix E for the official statement from the University president.)

The uproar over this case damaged the College's efforts to gain state funding to open a pharmacy school to increase the number of pharmacists in rural Kentucky. The money, $10 million, appropriated in 2006 by the Kentucky General Assembly, was to come from coal severance taxes designated for economic development for coal-producing counties. Following the announcement of the planned pharmacy school, a lawsuit was brought by the Kentucky Equality Federation. The lawsuit fueled rumors that the University discriminates against gay or lesbian students. Since accreditation for a pharmacy school would require the institution have a non-discrimination policy including sexual preference, the inference was that there was no reason to build the school since the prohibition against gay and lesbian students would prevent accreditation.

In 2008, a circuit judge ruled that a private institution which allows discriminatory practices in its admissions or expulsion policies cannot receive public money. The University appealed that decision, but a 2010 Kentucky Supreme Court ruling sided with the earlier determination, saying, "the Pharmacy School appropriation violates Section 189 [of the Kentucky Constitution], which prohibits public funding of 'any church, sectarian or denominational school . . . .'" A second award of $1 million had been requested to provide scholarships for students attending the proposed pharmacy school at UC so that the cost to those students would not exceed that of students attending the pharmacy school at UK. That award was also denied on the grounds that "the Pharmacy Scholarship Program violates Section 59, which prohibits special legislation."[5] In brief, the ruling was that public funds should not go to a private, church-supported institution for specific projects. The University was allowed, however, to keep $1.2 million from a federal grant awarded in 2009 to help complete a new health, exercise and wellness facility and construction of a new science building.[6]

A quick review of the letters UC received in response to the action taken with regard to the student suggests those who supported the decision were about as numerous as those who opposed it. A few of those writing were so strong in their belief that it was wrong for the student to have been expelled they requested the return of their donations; the treasurer refunded the money. Many, especially those who had attended the College, felt that Cumberland is the kind of place that develops strong and capable citizens prepared to make decisions for themselves based on their personal faith and understanding of governing rules and principles of behavior, and they were dismayed by the negative press surrounding the expulsion. As one wrote, "Mr. Johnson was not expelled for being gay. He was expelled for breaking the rules." In another letter a student pointed out how many of the rules (such as room checks) that he disliked when he was a student, but he knew if he did not obey them, he would be subject to expulsion, and he believed the College had his best interest at heart.

UC has maintained its position on premarital sex and on homosexuality, but in the most recent years there have not been recurring incidents related to that stance. The spring following the dismissal of the gay student, Soulforce, a pro-Gay and Lesbian rights group, demonstrated on the campus with minimum disruption. Again in the summer of 2009, the University uninvited a church group from Texas to spend time on the campus helping to build houses for the poor, supposedly because the group had openly supported homosexuality. Since that time, the issue has not publicly reappeared. Even if it is hard to agree with the position taken on matters related to sex—in whatever form—on the campus, it is not hard to respect the right to honor one's beliefs based on his or her understanding of the Bible. As Wheelan said, ". . . Everyone knows what it [UC] stands for." She continued by explaining, "Faith-based institutions like the University of the Cumberlands are critical to a world that sometimes seems to have no moral compass." Students in all colleges need more than academic content and training. As Derek Bok, former president of Harvard, indicated, students need a chance to shape their own values by knowing those of others.[7]

Faculty

In the 1970s and 1980s various scholars (including Bowen and Alexander Astin and Calvin Lee) predicted that by the late 1990s there would be major shortages of faculty for the vacancies across colleges that would be created by retirements, deaths, and transfers to nonacademic jobs. Given the length of time necessary to complete a doctoral degree, the predictions were that there would be a dearth of faculty with terminal degrees, especially in the humanities and social sciences, to replace those expected to leave colleges during the latter years of the twentieth century and the early decades of the twenty-first century. Those predictions have not come true; in fact, the opposite is true, at least for most small colleges. In recent years, when there have been vacancies at colleges such as UC, with the exception of a few fields (such as nursing), there has been a plethora of applicants—in part because colleges are filling many of their vacancies with adjuncts and new technologies are reducing the numbers of faculty necessary. Vacancies are being covered in ways unanticipated by the early studies: retirements, deaths, and transfers are taking place, but few of the vacated positions are being filled by traditional full-time, tenure-track faculty.

Despite the fact that there are many people qualified to teach as full-time, tenure-track faculty, budget cuts force many colleges to turn to adjuncts. According to a recent study, 47 percent of all faculty today are adjuncts.[8] Although it is often hard to find qualified people willing to serve as adjunct faculty in rural areas, it is not impossible; faculty at one college sometimes serve as adjuncts at another for extra pay. A new president at Union College in eastern Kentucky once called Taylor and asked where he found adjunct faculty. At that time Taylor's response was that he seldom used adjuncts. The Union president called Alice Lloyd College and was told that college did not use adjuncts. He called Eastern Kentucky University and asked where that university found adjunct faculty for the extension center it had established near Union College. The response was "We use faculty from Union College." Colleges located in rural areas find hiring qualified adjunct faculty far more problematic than do colleges in the more metropolitan areas, but UC's location on I-75 makes it more accessible to adjuncts than many such colleges.

Many circumstances impact the pool of faculty for colleges like Cumberland. According to the research study mentioned above, Americans with bachelor's degrees are increasingly becoming aware of how few faculty positions are available at the college level and fewer are seeking the Ph.D. with an eye toward teaching. The good news is that those who entered the market in the 1980s and 1990s have enabled schools such as UC to hire faculty with strong credentials that, in the past, might have landed them positions in major universities at high salaries. UC has focused on hiring those who know their subject matter but also know the students likely to attend a small rural college and their learning styles and can nurture all aspects of the students' lives, not just their intellectual capacities. As a result of the factors resulting in many new faculty for few positions, as well as the result of carefully matching applicants to institutional mission, today UC has—as many of those consulted indicated—an incredibly qualified and committed-to-teaching pool of faculty.

Sara Ash, a professor of biology, is typical. Ash was a student at UC and graduated in 1993. She went to Texas A&M for her master's and doctoral degrees—one of the largest universities in the nation. Then she returned to teach at UC in 2000 and was struck by how much had changed since her undergraduate years. She said that when she returned, she could clearly see the institution's vision and welcomed the opportunity to be a part of it. Obviously, faculty at UC do not have access to the resources that those at Texas A&M have, but Ash feels that she generally receives the supplies and equipment she needs. Like others I spoke with at UC, she finds the University a good place to be in an era where so many small private institutions are struggling to survive and so many public universities are reducing their numbers of faculty because of state budget cuts.

Several faculty consulted mentioned the opportunities for professional development provided directly by UC. Also, since UC is a member of the ACA, UC faculty can apply for grants to attend conferences, seminars, and institutes related to their disciplines and for fellowships to conduct research for as long as two years at a major research facility. UC itself offers a variety of travel and research experiences for faculty and the opportunity to serve in various administrative positions. Tom Fish, who moved from the UC English department to his role as Associate Dean of Academic Affairs, came from undergraduate study at Iowa State and the MA program and doctoral program in English at the University of Kansas. He taught at Iowa State for three years and then came to UC—intending, like many who came to teach at UC, to stay a short while, and, like many others, he has stayed much longer for good reasons: a commitment to serving Appalachia and providing opportunities to those in need. When I spoke with him, Fish said that he realizes that "there has been a generational shift in faculty today and people move around a lot now," but he "appreciates the opportunities at UC for professional growth."[9] He clearly finds administrative work challenging and rewarding. Moving into administrative roles is an opportunity that many once faculty have found, to the surprise of some of their colleagues, enjoyable and rewarding.

When UC is considering applicants for vacancies in academic fields, credentials, especially the Ph.D, are important; of the 118 full-time faculty, 83 have terminal degrees. However, UC does not try to recruit "trophy professors." What the College has found to be as important as academic credentials is familiarity with the region—its isolation as well as its beauty and its beliefs. Berea College, just north of UC, holds bus tours across eastern Kentucky to familiarize new faculty and staff with the culture of the region. This tour includes stops at sites in rural communities such as churches, community centers, settlement schools, and health clinics to highlight the background from which most of the students come. The approach UC has taken is to hire those already familiar with the Appalachian lifestyle—its commitment to family and the church, its education and health issues. Many of the UC faculty grew up in rural communities like those in Kentucky and Tennessee, and roughly 25 percent hold undergraduate degrees from Cumberland College itself.

The story of Early's affiliation with the University reflects many of the characteristics that have proved, if not essential, at least highly important to success as a faculty member there. Early's story illustrates one of the practices administrators at Cumberland College have found beneficial— "growing their own" faculty:

> I grew up within 200 yards of the college, at that time a two-year college. My elementary and high schools were literally across the street, so I knew many students and faculty at the college. My mother was the grade school supervisor, and the president of the college at that time, J.M. Boswell, asked her to be a faculty member in the education department.

> It was just assumed that I would move across the street to continue my education after graduating from high school. There I found, what I later realized, an amazing group of dedicated teachers. They were dedicated to their students and demanded excellence from

us. As I moved forward on my educational journey, I found out just how great these people really were. I was amazed at how well my friends and I were prepared for graduate studies. At the end of my graduate work in mathematics at the University of Tennessee, my mentor and mathematics professor at Cumberland came to Knoxville, and he, along with President Boswell, asked me to return. I became a part of the faculty in the fall of 1969.

By this time, the college had become a four-year institution, and the college had employed many new faculty members in order to meet the demands of the expanded curriculum. While these new people were wonderful Christians, they were not the caliber of faculty I had encountered while I was a student at Cumberland.[10]

Early's assessment of faculty in place when he returned to the campus to teach reflects concerns that he and Taylor had by the time Boswell retired. It appeared that the College was headed toward becoming a Bible college instead of a strong liberal arts college. Once Taylor was the president and Early was a vice president, their major goal was to assure students access to the best possible faculty—those who were Christian and committed to the region and its students but also were well versed in their academic disciplines.

Wake, Vice President for Institutional Advancement, as well as Taylor's chief assistant or "gate-keeper," once told me that it is obvious within a short period of time if a new faculty member is going to fit into the UC culture and stay: if a new employee stays for two years, she can be reasonably sure he or she will spend his or her years of professional life at the University. Such faculty can understand the students coming from the region—their weaknesses as well as their strengths. Several of the faculty questioned admitted that initially they had come with the intention of staying only a few years but the job market and the academic culture have kept them in their positions at Cumberland—and they seem sincerely appreciative of the opportunities they have there. Todd Yetter, Chair of the Biology Department, is a good example. Moving from a large city to Williamsburg, Yetter and his wife missed the diversity of opportunities available in the metropolitan area. Yet the longer they stayed at Cumberland College, the more friends they made and the more they "came to appreciate the school and the region."[11]

Heilman pointed out that Taylor's "heart and head are committed to the doctrines of the Baptist Church, and he is not embarrassed to promote those values. He has engaged others of like disposition; he does not have faculty or staff trying to make the institution what it is not." Heilman has "witnessed other small colleges established to serve the poor try to make the institution fit the mold of the privileged East Coast elite colleges, but Taylor "adheres to the true history of the college with relative intensity: he is proud to be what the college is instead of trying to be what it is not," and the faculty and staff work with him to serve this goal.

Taylor, in one of his numerous speeches, commented on those with whom the president has to be "a good fellow": "state legislators, congressmen, senators, the State Department, the denomination, the civic clubs, the community, alumni, the foundation and corporation world, and so on." It is interesting to note that there is no specific mention of the faculty in that statement. Even though he is clearly involved in the life of the institution and accessible (the door to his office is seldom closed), Taylor believes in maintaining distance between himself and the faculty and staff on which the operations of the institution depend. He once said that **one of the greatest stresses of the college presidency is "the necessity of keeping one's distance."**[12] This philosophy is endorsed by various scholars in the field: ". . . Productivity tends to be higher under leaders who maintain social and psychological distance between themselves and their followers."[13] Respect seems to be easier if we do not know a person so well the illusions they create can be destroyed: "The higher the perceived status . . . of the leaders, the more likely the group is to revere and accept him or her."[14]

Susan Pierce, a former president and author of a recent book of advice for presidents, takes a different stance, insisting that "most presidents thrive on the interaction they have with members of the campus community . . . ." She believes that "getting to know students or colleagues can be one of the most positive aspects" of life on the campus, that fund-raising is more rewarding when the president has "close, personal relationships with both the donors and those on campus who will benefit from the gifts."[15] And I have known many of the ACA presidents to make special efforts to communicate and collaborate with faculty, staff and students, inviting them to their homes for informal dinners and conversations as well as attending campus events with them. However, I have also seen numerous situations where presidents who have developed a close rapport with their faculty have given faculty the impression that virtually all institutional decisions are dependent on their input, and it is hard for the president to make decisions critical to the progress of the institution in the timeframe such decisions often require. One president once complained to me that his faculty were "offering suggestions" about his fund-raising practices, implying that they had more understanding of the intricacies of that work than he had—despite the fact that he had tried to stay out of matters related primarily to curricula and pedagogy. I have witnessed colleges where the faculty seem to be comfortable appearing diametrically opposed to whatever position their president takes on any issue, and, as a result of what seems resistance to change and/or resistance to seeing the president be successful, little progress is made at the institution toward any goal. Even Moody's, whose global economic analyses on risk in the market are used by major corporations and government agencies in making investment decisions, has cautioned about the increasing tension between administrators who need to develop strategies to improve the position of their institutions in the academic market and faculty who often resist change regardless of the reason for it.[16]

Taylor frequently emphasizes in his presentations that he believes **a president's maintaining distance between himself and the faculty and staff is "the most important key to success . . . ."** Several faculty mentioned that they seldom see Taylor; he may attend a faculty-staff dinner and once a year he speaks to the entire faculty about "how things are going." But, while faculty might like to build a personal relationship with their president, what the faculty at UC seem to appreciate most about him is his effectiveness with constituents outside the institution; they realize that his ability to raise money for the University depends on his time and attention spent on those outside agencies and individuals. Those working on the campus appreciate his appearances at campus games and other events but do not seem bothered by his absence when he is not present. They may prefer he be off campus raising money instead of enjoying a campus event. And many mentioned that what they appreciate most about President Taylor is that he does not micromanage the classrooms.

One faculty member did mention the negative aspect of keeping the president and his work so private; her comment was that it takes a long time for a person to appreciate Taylor's assets when they only hear about them from second- or third-hand sources. Another person commented that while most people on the campus realize the stress that leading an institution like UC must create and understand the distance that seems to exist between the president and employees, it is unfortunate that so many do not personally know Taylor's many good qualities as an individual. They do seem to know, however, that their president does not believe in using this distance between him and them to abuse his power. In advising other presidents Taylor has warned, **"Don't use raw power. Use persuasion, coax, beg, plead, cajole, compromise, but use raw power as the last type of persuasion."**[17]

Even though all on the campus know who is in charge of the institution, they also seem to know that institutional decisions made are based on what is in the best interest of the University and its students. One faculty member commented that there are times when she has "scratched her head" at the choices being made for the institution, but she takes comfort in knowing that what is important to her is what is happening in the classroom. Julie Tan, who leads the Chemistry Department, said that she reminds herself of a Chinese saying when she does not understand decisions being made by the president: "He has eaten more salt than I have eaten rice."[18] In short, she knows that he has more experience at running a college than she has.

Another of the ACA colleges, Tusculum, faced a major crisis in the late 1980s. The president there credits much of the turnaround of that college to the faculty and their creative (and exhausting) work on the college curriculum—a calendar change which meant the offering of one course at a time. The faculty took on the transition and "the momentum that came from a sense of ownership" helped to carry that college through some difficult years.[19] It appears that at UC the faculty have the same sense of owning their courses. All Taylor expects of the faculty is strong ethical, academic and behavioral standards, and he is willing to leave the decisions related to academic content and pedagogies to those in the trenches of the classrooms.

Taylor says that he has only fired one professor in all his years as president. Other separations have been through exit strategies, such as resignation or appointment to other positions. The College has bought out contracts, moved people from full to part-time, and provided special incentives for people to leave when the board was forced by changing economic issues to "right-size."[20] All faculty, those on tenure and those not on tenure, receive annual contracts, but salaries for the year are not finalized until fall enrollments are final.

Early observed that Taylor's tendency to avoid small talk, to get "to the point of a meeting in five minutes," often leads faculty to believe he is not interested in them or their situations. There is lots of evidence to contradict this impression; Taylor's staff noted that he remembers every discussion with faculty and generally acts to address issues brought to his attention quickly.[21] Wake can tell of many times when a faculty member has come to Taylor's office with a request in hand and by the time the faculty member has left the building, the request is on its way through the channels to approval.[22] One story about his prompt response to a need is about a student who, Taylor learned from a faculty member, needed transportation to Knoxville to interview for admission to the doctoral program in chemistry at the University of Tennessee. Taylor simply gave the student his car and his credit card. Today that student is a successful graduate of that doctoral program. However, as Wake explains, today everything has become so systematized that generally people know where to direct a request without having to bring it to the president.

President Taylor clearly admires his faculty and their work, but he knows that faculty have many criticisms of presidents and that some are contradictory. **"If the president balances the budget, he is stingy; however, if he runs a deficit, he is irresponsible. If another president maintains distance, he is perceived as being aloof; however, the president who dives into campus social life and becomes personally involved with faculty is seen as interfering."**[23] While I did not find any UC faculty who talked about wanting higher raises and lower teaching loads (typically the two top items on the wish list of faculty at ACA colleges), the Associate Dean of Academic Affairs indicated that he does know from faculty that they would like to have more opportunities to involve their students in research and more time to devote to each course and every student. I suspect some do blame the president when dissatisfied and think life on other campuses is better than on theirs. But none questioned were ready to complain; they seem to realize the benefits they enjoy, and they know—like so many in the field recognize—that Taylor deserves most of the credit for the University's relatively strong financial standing and much of the credit for the good reputation it enjoys. Yet the president also accepts the inevitable criticisms, no matter how unfair or even brutal they may be. Taylor knows, **"Criticism is always more prevalent than plaudits"**[24]—that he is expected to accept the blame for problems and share the praise for successes.

Even anticipating frustrating criticisms, Taylor has questions he asks himself every few years: **"(1) Have I made the college give better service to the students? (2) Is the faculty better than the one I inherited? (3) Does the college have a better reputation than it had . . . ? (4) Is the college better known? (5) Is the physical plant better? (6) Is there greater emphasis on values and learning?"**[25] While his answer to each question has repeatedly been a resounding "yes," he is quick to deflect credit from himself: in an interview he said, **"It would be incorrect to give me the credit. The recognition comes largely because of the expertise, the devotion and hard work of our faculty, staff, students, and the support given to our work by our alumni, trustees, and friends across America who have given generously of their time, talents and resources."**[26]

It is clear that the central administrators and trustees respect the faculty and their right to make judgments related to their departments and disciplines, and that the institution makes every effort to reward faculty for their work and commitment and to supply them with the resources needed in their teaching. Faculty in the sciences were the most vocal about how well supported they felt. Clearly, the University has reasons to want those associated with the sciences to feel they have what they need to teach well: roughly 30 percent of all students applying to UC express interest in majoring in a science field, and the institution has several new graduate programs related to the health sciences. One faculty member who teaches science courses said that she never has to worry about having the supplies she needs for her labs: "If I need it I can get it."[27]

It is also clear that decisions related to operating the institution remain with the president and board. When Taylor moved into the presidency, there were some questions about who had tenure and who did not have it. Once that question was resolved, a formal procedure for awarding tenure was established by the board and with the blessing of the faculty, who wanted it clearly understood that tenure is an act of validation and not simply a perfunctory award. Still, the University allows no more than 50 percent of a division to be tenured to avoid the duress that could result in time of financial stress when budgets may need to be reduced by cutting faculty and/or staff positions. Some faculty consider such limits a problem in attracting new faculty, but apparently those who have been on a non-tenure track at the University for many years do not feel a lack of security in their positions.

When UC faculty make comparisons between their salaries and benefits and teaching loads and professional development opportunities and those of faculty at other private colleges in the region, they can see that they are fortunate. Salaries are comparable: at the rank of full professor, the 2010-2011 salary average was about $52,000 while salaries at other private colleges in eastern Kentucky were between $40,000 and $57,000. For all other ranks, UC faculty salaries were slightly above those at the other nearby private colleges or universities.[28]

Maintaining good benefits, as well as establishing good salaries for faculty, is a major focus for the University. The retirement contribution is a 5 percent match of the faculty member's salary, and faculty can contribute as much as the maximum allowed by the University's plan. When the institution had to reduce the percentage contributed for retirement to assure a balanced budget, the board instituted a tuition remission program for the children and spouses of faculty, increased pay for off-campus teaching and increased travel allowances. In the past three years, faculty have received no raise, a raise of 1 percent and a raise of 2 percent, but benefits have increased: a Flexible Spending Plan, dental insurance and a vision program have been added. As health insurance premiums have increased, the University has held the amounts charged to employees steady. And in 2013 with the opening of the campus health clinic, employees have access to the campus physician. Through work of the academic deans and vice-presidents, as well as fund-raising by the development staff, faculty at UC have continued to enjoy professional development opportunities, such as travel to workshops and release time for planning new courses, learning new computer or pedagogical skills, or advancing content knowledge.

I can remember a time when I was working at UK, and the budget was so tight that faculty and staff on the campus were forbidden to charge long-distance telephone calls to office accounts even if the calls were business related. I can remember when the ACA was trying to help faculty at the member colleges get computers; some faculty at some ACA colleges complained they would just like to have a telephone nearby. Things do not seem ever to have been so depressed at Cumberland.

An excerpt from a speech to the faculty and administrative staff reflects Taylor's efforts on their behalf:

> **I am aware that salaries are not what they should be, that retirement is meager, that fringe benefits are modest. I know that inflation is eating away at your paycheck. I appreciate the dedication and devotion of our faculty and staff. I know that the kitchen is hot (literally, and needs air conditioning) . . . that we do not have the equipment we need. But . . . united we can begin to change the situation . . . . Every dollar saved is a dollar that can be returned in a more beautiful or better maintained campus or in other direct or indirect benefits. I . . . try to do everything I can to improve our lot. We are all "in the same boat" and the sea is stormy.**[29]

Robert Maynard Hutchins, dean at the Yale Law School followed by 16 years as president at the University of Chicago, said that a major administrator "must be a trouble-maker; for every change in education is a change in the habits of some members of the faculty."[30] Certainly there must be some faculty at UC who think of Taylor as making trouble for them every time the board expands programs or campuses or has to terminate a program; there are some who dream of moving from Cumberland to a college or university where teaching loads are two or three courses per semester instead of four or more and salaries are at least 20 percent higher. But what has most amazed me about the faculty I have talked with at Cumberland is their remarkably positive attitudes. When questioned about how they reacted to announcements that there would be no salary increases for the coming year, the general view was that faculty knew they were lucky they were not losing their jobs instead of a raise. When I talked to one who had recently had a grant request to a major foundation rejected, her response was, "But I learned so much in the process of preparing the application." When I questioned faculty about teaching loads that often exceed 12 hours per semester and often include three to four preparations, their response was generally, "But I only have a few students in the upper division courses." They seem to make a little good news go a long way and to find the brightest spot possible in bad news.

Although the general media coverage for higher education today might lead one to believe that most faculty are discontent complainers, UC is certainly not the only college with cooperative faculty. Hidden in various stories about small private colleges are examples of the admirable qualities of many faculty: on the first page of Keller's book about Elon University, there is a quote by a new academic dean there reflecting the character of faculty and staff even prior to the turnaround from surviving to thriving: "There are almost no petty feuds or intrigues here. Most faculty care for the students and teach imaginatively; they support each other and actually like the administration. And the faculty have renovated their own general education program. The administrators, too, are a talented, collaborating team. There is a very, very strong sense of community here at Elon."[31] The same seems true at UC.

When questions are raised, such as why there is no faculty senate or only two general faculty meetings per semester, they usually come from new faculty. Those who have been at the University for a long time seem grateful when there are administrative issues they do not need to consider and when the problem is too few meetings—instead of too many. From my earlier research on a number of other colleges, it is clear that sometimes faculty are so intimidated by the central administrators, they are hesitant to make critical comments about them. At UC, however, it truly seems that faculty are grateful that the central administrators stay busy assuring the financial stability of the institution and attracting a growing population of students, and that the strong academic reputation of the University is in the control of the faculty.

Given the location of UC in rural Kentucky, employment opportunities outside the campus are so limited that the University has attempted to address that problem by allowing faculty couples to teach there, some in the same department. About 15 percent of those teaching are married to another UC faculty member, and there are a number of couples where one is faculty and the other is staff. Similarly, a number of those employed are children of faculty. Perhaps one story will illustrate the freedom the faculty seem to feel about determining departmental practices and their concern for others on the campus. When I visited the chair of one division, the woman who serves as the receptionist for the department had a baby about three months old sitting in an infant seat on her desk. When I asked about it, she explained that the baby is hers and that the department has allowed her to reduce her working hours to 20 per week and students are serving in her place for the other 20—and she can bring the baby to work during her shifts. I asked how long she would be allowed to bring the infant to work; the response was "until there is a problem with my doing so."

When recruiting new faculty, those interviewed said that they quickly admit that salaries seem low when compared to those at many other colleges in other locations, but many costs are lower in the local region: housing is inexpensive, and the University itself provides some faculty housing. There are many other benefits: the aesthetic beauty of the area, the fact that the campus is isolated but just off I-75 so reaching Knoxville, Tennessee, takes only about an hour and Lexington, Kentucky, is less than two hours away. The institution has "a heart for teaching," and there are lots of enticements encouraging the continual improvement of teaching skills—including stipends and summer immersion grants. Although there is no sabbatical program managed by the University, the fact that UC is a member of the

ACA means faculty are eligible for grants of up to $30,000/year for faculty projects designed to improve a teacher's knowledge and expertise in his or her field. One piece of information that is used to attract new faculty is that the reputation of the academic programs at UC seems to grow stronger each year.

Len Schlesinger, President of Babson College, says that "Colleges need to . . . position themselves for the new economic reality by focusing on what they can do best."[32] What UC seems to do best is "care." One of the best "selling points" of UC is that the institution is one in which people care about one another, students are generally well behaved, and faculty are well respected. Cockrum says that what sets the UC faculty apart from many at other universities is that they have "caring hearts," that while they are well versed in research what they most appreciate is seeing "the light come on in individuals' eyes" when they first understand some concept being taught.[33] When students are asked what they most like about UC, many mention how the faculty really want all their students to succeed. They talk about the small class sizes, how professors not only know your name but they don't mind impromptu office visits, being called on the phone or being contacted by email. One claimed that the faculty will not let any student fail if he or she is willing to spend more time studying than socializing. Students comment about how faculty will tutor them outside the classroom, spend a lot of time being sure every student in the class understands the materials, encourage them to go to graduate school, or help them find employment in their fields of choice.

To illustrate the commitment of faculty, Susan Weaver, Director of Teaching, Learning, and Assessment, gives an example of a physics professor who taught an advanced class without compensation to enhance one student's chance of success at one of the best graduate schools in his major. She knows faculty who attend special study events held late at night and spend time outside the classroom encouraging students to participate in internships and international travel. She has been impressed since she came to the campus in 2005 by how well everyone works together, formally and informally: "One does not see the strong territorial boundaries that one sees in some institutions because units tend to be small and need to work together to accomplish goals. Cooperation and collaboration build bonds." Weaver also emphasizes how faculty anticipate and address needs of students that might not have been anticipated, inviting students into their homes for dinners and special events, taking birthday cakes to dorm rooms, and even giving students money for books and other supplies when it is obvious they are in financial distress.[34]

At one conference where ACA faculty were on the program with some from Harvard, the Harvard folks complimented the cooperation across the ACA colleges, pointing out that at Harvard the philosophy is "Every boat on its own bottom." Faculty there give little attention to causes that are beyond their own discipline. At UC faculty not only care about those in disciplines and departments across the campus, they often care about those across other colleges in the region and beyond. The ACA was established on the belief that faculty across small campuses can benefit from collaborating with faculty at other campuses—small and large, and many of the Cumberland College faculty were very active in the organization during my 25 years of leading it. This spirit of cooperation and collaboration among faculty and among the faculty and their students—of caring for others—is a primary principal on which UC was established and has thrived. As Pat Summitt, the former highly successful women's basketball coach at the University of Tennessee, said, "Students don't care how much the faculty know if they don't know how much the faculty care."[35] At UC the caring extends across all levels of the campus and beyond.

Staff

At the same time that Taylor tries to avoid false expectations by stressing the realities of the financial shape of the University, he has worked to improve the remunerations and benefits for staff as well as for faculty. The University has admitted hourly employees to the retirement program, consistently worked to improve life insurance and hospitalization coverage for all staff, and provided tuition remission for staff and their families as well as for faculty and their families. Each year five or six of the University's staff graduate from there.

Faculty at other colleges often complain that the number of administrative staff is three or four times the number of full-time faculty and sometimes their salaries are similar. Taylor has kept the number of administrative staff at UC relatively low (and he has not resorted to having administrators that teach classified as faculty in those counts). There are 118 full-time faculty and 180 full-time staff in administrative offices. Although these numbers do not include 119 contract employees hired by companies providing security, foodservice, facilities management and the bookstore,[36] since most staff make less than faculty, the percentage of the budget devoted to staff versus that for faculty is not reflected by the counts above.

As changes have been made to employee policies, Taylor has tried to assure the continuity of those existing which have helped to boost morale as well as maintain equality and fairness. No one can deny that change is a constant and institutions need to change to assure continued quality, substance and character. Taylor admits that sometimes changes are made not only to make progress but also to adapt for survival Those who work at UC seem to recognize the benefits of holding a position at an institution which is more financially secure and progressive than many, and they recognize that in many cases security and progress require frequent changes. Another thing staff seem to appreciate is that UC represents an equal opportunity community with ability being criteria for promotion rather than age, sex, race/ethnicity, or length of service.[37]

When Taylor was serving on the ACA board, he offered what seemed an uncommonly clear understanding of staff. When an evaluator from one of the major foundations funding the ACA concluded that morale among ACA staff seemed low, Taylor's response was that of course morale was low; it was late January—a time when the weather is "dark, cold, wet and as a consequence people are suffering with cabin fever and at times irritable and short with each other . . . ; Christmas has come and gone and now the bills are arriving . . . ; New Years has come and gone and people are already breaking their New Year's Resolutions . . . ; spring break is still some time off . . . ."[38] When ACA staff seemed upset about my creating the position of vice-president, he responded, "Of course the staff was upset; you were putting someone between them and you, and they saw this change as a demotion." Taylor explained his experience in a similar situation: "During Boswell's administrator everyone reported to him, something which changed the day I became president [and named several vice-presidents]; thus, almost everyone experienced a demotion in position, which no one likes . . . . **I find people don't fear change as much as they fear where they will fit in among the new change.**"[39] His awareness of and sensitivity to the feelings of general staff helped me to understand the reactions of those in my office.

And staff at UC seem infused with the same positive attitudes as faculty. Taylor once called one of the campus offices when he was driving through the mountains and mentioned that it was pouring rain; the response of the staff person was, "Maybe you'll see a rainbow."[40]

Students

Students at UC reflect both the region and the institution. Roughly half come from central Appalachia, most from Kentucky and Tennessee. They are both products of the culture and shapers of it. And the University realizes the importance of cultural fit in the recruitment and retention of students. In *The Innovative University*, the authors make a case for preserving the traditional college campus: "Young college students . . . need an environment in which they can not only study but also broaden their horizons and simply 'grow up.'"[41] For students who come from rural communities with little diversity in population and few opportunities for travel outside their local county, the campus is particularly important in providing life-changing resources of culturally diverse populations, intellectually stimulating professors, libraries, and laboratories. One of the goals UC claims is that it helps those who view themselves as ordinary to realize they can be extraordinary.

In 2013, National Public Broadcasting did a report on how elite colleges cannot recruit low-income students, even with scholarships that include not only tuition but also the cost of room and board (and sometimes even funding for flights home). The researchers concluded that even though there is a large pool of talented, low-income students, such students are so scattered across a wide, sparsely populated geographic region that it is almost impossible to find them; they do not belong to peer groups applying to highly selective colleges or have access to any of the pipelines leading to such placements.[42] Numerous respondents to that broadcast reflect what seems a more plausible explanation:

> I grew up in a small farming community in rural Wisconsin, did very well in school, and pretty much had my pick of colleges. I didn't even consider attending the Ivy schools. It wasn't the distance, it

wasn't the cost, it wasn't the challenge. I felt they were smug places filled with intellectual one-upmanship. I felt culturally it wouldn't be the place for me, that it was the place for rich East coast kids. I know a number of people who did make the jump out there and about half returned after the first year. They said they were socially outcast because they didn't have stories of European vacations or yacht club memberships, nor could they drive their trust fund BMW to the Hamptons for spring break. Let alone the snobby jokes about public school and thinking the Olive Garden was a nice diner. It's no fun being constantly and bluntly told you are common and poor.

One who responded to the NPR segment even offered "a short list of reasons why low-income students may not flock to the Ivy Leagues":

1.) Selling themselves short. Many low-income students do not know an Ivy League grad and are not dreaming big enough to see themselves in that role.

2.) Guidance Counselors. I would suspect that most guidance counselors at large low-income schools are more occupied with troubled students rather than the Ivy entrance requirements for a select few.

3.) Distance. Being low-income does not allow for a great deal of travel . . . . Many students' world exposure has been limited to their locality due to a lack of financial means. Moving across the nation to the Northeast where you don't know a soul is quite intimidating . . . if you [have] never left your state.

4.) Cost of living. Big cities are expensive. A low-income family may find it difficult to support the increased cost in food and transportation, never mind socializing with the exorbitant tastes of your upper-income peers.

5.) Social-economic cultural differences. It's going to be hard to connect to your upper-income peers . . . . Try trading stories about working in a gas station when you were 17 with someone who spent every summer shopping in Paris.

Some reflected on the fact that putting someone into a setting where he or she is uncomfortable is a good way to encourage him or her to leave college.[43]

Many of the students at UC are from families living at or near the poverty rate: 50 percent of the students are Pell Grant Eligible,[44] and roughly 40 percent are the first in their families to attend college—38 percent in 2011 and 44 percent in 2012.[45] For such students, colleges like UC are a good step toward emotional, social, and intellectual adulthood; without such colleges many would be left behind to depend on welfare to survive. Such colleges allow a level of comfort in which the student can thrive without significant fear of ridicule, without loss of confidence. For some students UC is a good choice among several; it is a college close to home staffed by people from their culture and faculty who understand their strengths and weaknesses and have the patience and persistence to adapt pedagogies to match the learning styles of the students. For others, it is simply their only choice; Appalachian parents are noted for their desire to keep their children near home. At UC, the typical student's home is within an 80-mile radius of the campus.

The mission that established the College and has sustained it—providing educational opportunities for disadvantaged populations—promises to serve the institution even more in the future as the number of low income students continues to grow. Just as UC has kept the curriculum relevant to serve these students, it has stayed near the forefront in strategies for recruiting them. When, in the 1990s, the ACA annual meeting for presidents included a presentation by Dehne on recruiting students, he talked about web-based recruitment of students in the Northeast. He pointed out that colleges in the Northeast were charging tuitions that were significantly higher and the educational offerings were not necessarily better than those at the Appalachian colleges. UC was already engaged in such recruitment strategies and had monitored the success of the various approaches to recruiting students across a wide geographic area by using the web. What UC and other ACA colleges have learned is that the students most likely to enroll at a small, rural, denominationally affiliated, reasonably priced college are those from the local region.

Generally, the policy that seems to have worked the best for UC in hiring faculty at least familiar with the region if not from it works well in the recruitment of students: those most likely to stay and benefit from the experiences UC offers are those most comfortable with the Appalachian culture—its isolation, its beauty, its emphasis on family and the church. Of the over 4000 students (including online and residential) enrolled in the fall of 2012, 45 percent were from the Appalachian region, as defined by the Appalachian Regional Commission in Washington, DC.

Colleges like UC teach young people who come from families with low incomes and limited exposure to multiple cultures, as one resident of the region put it, "how to pass for normal, how to fit in, and most of all, how to keep folks from knowing I had no idea what I was doing while I figured out how to do it." In her autobiography, *Creeker: A Woman's Journey*, Linda Scott DeRosier, who eventually received a doctorate degree and taught at several major universities, describes her decision to go to college: ". . . I really wanted to get married immediately . . . [but] at that time, Kentucky administered standardized tests to all high school seniors, and some combination of my not missing anything on that test and the fact that I had a very clear view of the toes of my shoes [i.e., she did not have big breasts that might attract a husband] was responsible for my finding myself in college. I received scholarship offers from a number of schools, but, since I didn't know the difference between Smith and Smith Junior College of Knoxville, I applied the only standard I knew—distance . . . ." DeRosier chose a college within a 50-mile radius of her home. When her father took her to the college, she saw him cry for only the second time in her life: ". . . My daddy envisioned the fork in the road right there. Education, if it takes, changes the inside of our heads so that we do not see the same world we previously saw."[46] A small private liberal arts college near her home served DeRosier well; and Cumberland has done the same for thousands of students.

Yet, for students who do come into the region from outside it, the experiences of UC often transform their lives in unexpected ways. UC, in recruiting students to the region, has found that such students often remain in the region even after they graduate. In a study of alumni conducted for the ACA member colleges, one interesting finding was that students from outside Appalachia who attend a private college in Appalachia are more likely to stay in the region after graduation than those who come to Appalachia and attend a public university.[47] In many cases, students who come to study in the region stay to try to help improve the socio-economic conditions they find during their years as undergraduates. Since one of Taylor's concerns has always been "brain-drain," he takes pride in the fact that so many of the graduates (as many as 65 percent) stay in the region after graduation.

Although the retention rate (over 60 percent between freshman and sophomore years) and graduation rate (over 40 percent) are higher than at many comparable colleges, the regional culture, especially the strong ties to family, contributes to the dropout rate: someone in the family gets sick and the children are needed to help with work at home; family members accuse the student home for a visit of "getting above your upbringing"; the boyfriend or girlfriend back home is a powerful draw. I once heard a dean of students say at an orientation for parents of the freshman class, "If you have been thinking about getting a divorce as soon as the kids were out of the house, wait four more years." At UC problems at home seem to be about as frequent a reason for leaving college as financial problems. Sometimes the reasons a student leaves college are the result of emotional trauma more serious than the financial deficits that are the major issue in such cases at most campuses.

UC takes seriously responsibility to the students recruited to the campus. Students are encouraged to take a broad range of undergraduate courses, and double majors are encouraged to broaden the options for employment the graduates will have. UC recently reduced the number of courses required in the general education program by ten hours so that students have more options in planning their course schedules and more time to devote to selected classes. Although developmental courses stopped being part of the curriculum after the proliferation of the community colleges, the University still provides peer tutoring and professor-led study sessions for those who enter with high expectations but little preparation. There are honors programs and academic teams for those who are ready to excel. There are special study sessions targeting athletes who need help with their courses, as well as clubs to help them learn to focus on their faith and obligations to others. There are programs for those who have the ability to succeed in college but have never developed some of the skills critical to that success, such as those related to studying and test taking. Approximately 30 percent of the UC students enter planning to major in STEM disciplines—science, technology, engineering and math—a percentage that is high in comparison to that at many colleges and universities and one which presents a challenge: sometimes even those who enter with good grades and test scores need help to be successful in such rigorous discipline areas. One student summed up what many seem to believe: "Faculty here won't let you fail if you do the work."

The University takes pride in the results obtained by administering various tests to freshmen (Measure of Academic Proficiency and Progress and/or the California Critical Thinking Disposition Inventory and the California

Critical Thinking Skills Test) and measuring those scores against ones gathered through testing at the junior level. For freshman, the average scores are "almost identical" to national norms, but the averages for juniors are higher than those in the reference group for UC in virtually every category.[48]

Mike Colegrove, Vice President for Student Services for the past 23 years, hears frequently that students find there is little to do outside of working, serving, and studying. Dehne quoted some students as saying that Wal-mart makes living in the area "bearable." Among the complaints that come to Colegrove's office are calls from the local Wal-mart about students playing hide-and-seek in the store. I was confused about what would attract college students to Wal-mart for a game of hide-and-seek until I learned that Wal-mart is about the only store open to the public 24 hours each day, and many late nights it becomes the social center for sleepless-in-Williamsburg students.

However, Colegrove and his staff work hard to provide recreational and social events for the entertainment of students, adding new ones frequently. He wanted to be sure that I understand that playing hide-and-seek in Wal-mart is not the only social activity available to the students. They have a variety of options in clubs and honor societies; new clubs can be created if there is a pool of students interested in forming and maintaining them. Those ongoing include the Academic Team, a member of the Kentucky College

Quick Recall League; the American Chemical Society Student Affiliates (not just for chemistry majors); Beta Beta Beta Honor Society, a national honor and professional society for biology majors; Campus Activity Board, which arranges recreational and social activities, including dances, films, etc; Campus Ambassadors, who assist admissions staff with recruitment activities and help freshmen adjust to college life; Council for Exceptional Children, which provides tutoring and other support services for area children; Cumberland Mentor Program, where UC students mentor local middle-school students in academic and athletic and social or service activities; Fellowship of Christian Athletes; Intramural Athletics; Mathematics and Physics Club; Patriot Adventure Club, which takes advantage of the numerous state and national parks and forests in the area with trips for hiking, camping, caving, canoeing, and white-water rafting and volunteers in environmentally related service projects; Residence Hall Council, students elected by peers to help with services related to residence-hall life; Rollins Rowdies, a student-formed group of loyal UC fans; Speech and Debate Team; Student Government Association, which provides the voice of the students through elected representatives and provides liaison between students and college officials; and the Swing Dance Society.[49] Other organizations focused on student life outside the classroom are explained in the section on community service.

In a typical semester, students have the opportunity to hear presentations by distinguished national speakers under a leadership program funded by Terry and Marion Forcht; and the office of Student Activities sponsors bands and/or vocalists or other entertainers, various picnics (such as the Paintball Picnics), movies, talent shows, Corn Hole contests, Murder Mystery nights, and other such events. One student commented on having the opportunity to be hypnotized by a mentalist who performed on the campus. Early in the semester there might be a different event every evening; later, during exam weeks, for example, the focus is likely to be on midnight brunches or food deliveries to the dorms for students studying. One student mentioned that while Williamsburg is a small town, the Student Government Association provides shuttles to and from Knoxville and Lexington. And the University has so many athletic teams that there is often a game to attend. As one student said, "You can always find something to do if you are creative and open to new ideas." But Colegrove stresses that if there are too many activities for the students, they often try to participate in all to the neglect of their work and service and academic responsibilities, so he and his staff help students understand the importance of balancing time spent on work and on play.[50]

Visitors to the campus frequently comment on how well behaved the students at UC seem, but the University is well aware that for many of them college is their first real experience away from family, and the University takes the responsibility of *in loco parentis* seriously. There are a variety of regulations and restrictions placed on the students, especially freshmen, and a variety of ways the University monitors their behavior. Convocations are required and students sign in to verify their presence. Although the University realizes that social media is a public forum and all postings are not factual, it monitors Facebook pages and Twitter feeds in order to try to address concerns before they become major issues across the campus. For example, when students started complaining about all the fried food the cafeteria served, the cooks began to offer more choices that were grilled or baked. When they complained that there was no place to go and study once the library closes at 10 pm, the coffee center started staying open until midnight. When a student complains about noise near his or her room, the residential director is notified. When a student complained about the computer service in his dorm, the director of information technology started "house calls," where he visits each dormitory regularly to hold open forums that give students a chance to indicate problems the campus computer system has.

When students are accused of major infractions of the rules, an effort is made by the student affairs office to counsel him or her before more serious disciplinary actions are taken. The various deans in the offices of Academic Affairs and Student Affairs work together to assure students delinquent in their course assignments and/or in their social behavior are provided with counseling. If students are found guilty of an infraction that warrants expulsion, they are usually allowed to withdraw from the institution.[51]

Despite the fact that the University does take its responsibility for *in loco parentis* seriously, some parents are not convinced that their children are receiving all the attention they need. A major problem for Colegrove is the "helicopter parents"—those who hover over their children, taking responsibility in a number of areas where the children should be learning to manage on their own or where a college would normally be expected to manage. The cell phone has fostered the development of such parents, allowing immediate contact between parents and children; according to one study, two of every five students are in daily (or more often) contact with their parents.[52] And according to Colegrove, in a typical week, he spends as much time talking with parents as he does with students. Fish expressed similar concerns about parents—about the frequency of their calls and visits. In some cases, parents simply want some assurance that the money they are paying for tuition is well spent and their child is behaving appropriately; in other cases they want to be sure concerns their children have with another student or a faculty member are being addressed. Fish said that he can often tell the moment that a parent realizes that his or her child has not been providing the full truth to those at home. But as Cumberland students are similar in many ways to those at other colleges, so parents of the Cumberland students are similar to other parents. In the study mentioned above, student affairs directors across campuses indicated that parental involvement in their children's lives and in college affairs has increased significantly in recent years.

Some students complain about the strong focus on the Christian faith, saying that a lot of campus programs are basically "mini-sermons." Others find the focus on faith critical to helping them develop as a whole person, not simply as an educated one. Dehne was consulting on the campus on September 11, 2001, and witnessed the strong Christian bearing that the students had when they held a memorial vigil for those who had died that day. He was impressed by how "clean-cut" the students were and "how open they were about their religious faith."

Colonel Colegrove, who served as President of Hargrave Military Academy for two years, was a student at Cumberland, graduating in 1971. In addition to years of military service, he has worked in a variety of capacities at the University—including as a director of admissions, registrar, and professor of education. He has not only seen changes over the years, he has been an active participant in many of them. And there are few complaints he has not heard. But he also sees the surveys of alumni reflecting what the University meant to them and how comfortable and secure they had felt as students on the campus. He agrees with the students who say that at UC "everybody cares for each other." And that makes a lot of difference when students are tempted to step outside the institutionally mandated confines.

International Students

African-American students comprise only 6.5 percent of the student body, and while that is a much larger proportion than in the local geographic region, the University focuses on increasing the cultural diversity on the campus by working to increase the number of African-Americans and the number of international students. Currently there are just over 100 international students from 33 different countries—a number that increases slightly each semester as the institution continues to strengthen recruitment efforts for such students. Most of the international students are from Brazil, China, the United Kingdom and Canada.[53]

Rick Fleenor, Dean of Chapel and Director of Church Relations, is also Director of International Relations. Like a number of those holding administrative positions at the University, he graduated from the College in business and attended Southern Baptist Theological Seminary in Louisville, Kentucky. Shortly after graduation from the seminary, he was recruited back to Cumberland. When he told Cumberland he could not move for several months because his wife was expecting their first child, the College offered to hold the position for him. This incident indicates one of the attractions to prospective employees. The president did not simply make an offer to Fleenor; he made it clear that Fleenor was sincerely wanted. Sometimes the intangible incentives are more important than the tangible ones. Fleenor came to UC in 1992 as Assistant to the President. This practice of hiring a person who is a good match for the administrative needs and giving him or her a title that can encompass various responsibilities is another Taylor tradition.

By 1994 Fleenor was given responsibility as Alumni Director and as Director for a music group which represented the University by performing in churches, and he also served as Director of International Programs, working with the 45-50 international students then on campus. By 2013 there were 125 such students enrolled for the fall and 100 for the spring. Today he is responsible for church relations, student convocations, and international students—recruiting them and helping them get acclimated to their new environment.

UC does not offer English as a Second Language because it is not accredited to offer such courses, but it does offer an English class to help the international students with their language skills. Graduation rate for these students is about the same as that for all students on the campus—about 40 percent graduate within five years. While UC does lose some foreign students to programs based in large cities where the multiple populations from across the world are likely to provide students a greater sense of the culture of their home countries, most surveyed find that the caring community at UC is special enough to make them feel at home. There are no separate dorms for international students, for student-athletes, or for any select group. The hope is that by integrating all residential students across the dorms the students will develop a global perspective not likely if those from countries outside the US or from cultures different from those typical for the region are segregated into different majors or residencies or activities.

Students who attend UC from other countries help to recruit new students when they return to their native lands; missionaries and alumni involved in international programs help, and coaches recruit through agents. The University sends some of its staff recruiters and consultants into various countries, and all these various approaches to recruiting have resulted in a strong pool of people helping internationally just as friends of the institution recruit locally; none are paid a commission based on numbers of students enrolled. Also, UC lists opportunities in various electronic resources, including scholarships for those from outside the US.

There have been a number of efforts to offer special events celebrating the cultures of the different groups represented on the campus, such as having a Chinese New Year's Celebration. But the University has found that the students from outside the US really want to be made a part of the collective institution and not set apart from it. What they most appreciate is what all UC students appreciate: a caring community, personalized attention from faculty and staff, the safe environment and free tutorials as needed. They find Williamsburg, Kentucky, different from the vision most often portrayed of American cities; a city block or so in New York City might have more residents than the whole city of Williamsburg, but those from countries outside the US seem to appreciate the differences.

In an effort to give American students more exposure to various cultures around the world, UC has increased opportunities for American students to travel to other countries by working with the ACA program located in Belize and by encouraging faculty to explore various international study programs where their students can learn first-hand about other cultures. There is not a specifically designated UC international studies program, but many of the students have opportunities to travel abroad through classes, research experiences, or service projects. One student, for example, recently worked with the St. Eustatius Center for Archaeological Research on St. Eustatius, Netherlands Antilles.[54]

Curriculum

Even in the early years with a small student body, the curriculum for the College "was broad in its offerings, and a real attempt was made to meet the needs of the young people of the area," most of whom were studying to be ministers, lawyers, or doctors: English, Latin, Greek, political science, philosophy, German, French, mathematics, physics and natural sciences—and a Normal Department devoted to preparing teachers.[55] The courses at Cumberland College evolved over the years, and as Wheelan explained in observing the success it has had, the University "has made programmatic changes to accommodate the realities of a sharply changing world." She could have added "dramatic" before "programmatic." UC has expanded the curriculum to include new models of teaching and learning and new programs leading to professional and graduate degrees while maintaining a focus on the liberal arts. Since those early years, a lot has changed in the philosophies governing what students need to know. As Bok said when he spoke about the core curriculum at Harvard, ". . . The major goal of the new Core was not to ensure a common grounding in knowledge and values but rather to impart common capabilities for acquiring knowledge . . . . The way things are taught matters more than what is taught."[56] And UC has changed and continues to change the way subjects are covered; today courses are taught in classrooms on campus, online so students can take a course from any location, and in combinations of on-campus and online.

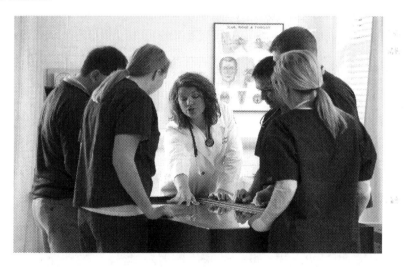

Cumberland long ago learned how to operate frugally, how not to anticipate income until it comes, how a mission-driven workforce can accomplish more than one driven by greed, how athletics are important to the development of the students but sports do not have to control the institution; and, perhaps most important, how continuing to update the curriculum is critical to both attracting students and serving them. As Cockrum says, "The four-year liberal arts traditional student is a smaller piece of the pie for such colleges [as UC], in part because there are fewer high school graduates." A lot of people have said what Cockrum believes drives much of the enrollment of today:

"The four-year liberal arts degree today is what the high school degree was 25 years ago. Students today come to college to get the skills that are the key to the gate of employment," and sometimes getting the job depends on having something different from or more than a bachelor's degree. Roughly 15 years ago, Zemsky ran a workshop for ACA presidents and their chief academic officers during which he presented statistics that indicated both students and their parents across the US saw preparation for a job as the number one reason for going to college. It is not just poor students in Appalachia who are going to college to qualify for productive employment. Today UC is working hard to prepare its students—traditional and non-traditional—for future employment opportunities as well as for a life of good citizenship.

In addition to a variety of courses leading to almost 40 different majors for undergraduates and opportunities for mentoring when students have difficulty with a course, the University is building a significant pool of courses providing continuing education after the bachelor's degree.

Graduate Programs

I heard both support and caution around the growth of online education on the UC campus. Faculty are supportive of the concept and recognize the role such courses can play in helping those not able to spend time on the campus—as well as students who may need more flexibility in their course scheduling than is typically available. But there is concern that the University is moving so fast into the world of online education that quality might suffer despite the efforts of the assessment office and the office handling academic affairs to monitor the classes. References were made to years past when the University had less than the stellar academic reputation of today and the years it took to overcome that reputation. Several faculty offered a plea to be sure that the University does not move so quickly into this new technological approach that its academic reputation might suffer as a result of offering courses that are not as strong as they might be. The graduate programs were the ones where most concern was expressed. Cockrum promises, "The University of the Cumberlands will continue to look at innovations in higher education that can assure quality and create new revenue streams" at the same time that such innovations increase the options for its graduates. This tension between "doing it now and doing it right" is probably the one case of concern I sensed where UC faculty and administrators might be at odds. Still, a major theme in interviews with faculty was their trust in Cockrum and his office to see that their concerns are heard and addressed.

The University tries to assure the same quality of instruction for online and in-class courses. Syllabi and learning outcomes measured by tests are the same, and often the same professors teach the online and the in-class courses. Part-time and adjunct faculty are monitored carefully and evaluated every semester. The University surveys all students every year, including those in the graduate programs. The 2011-2012 survey of graduate students had a total of 668 respondents, over 90 percent of whom originally enrolled in the UC program with just under 10 percent having transferred from another graduate program. About half of the students were full-time, and many continued to work fulltime while attending the graduate program. Most were seeking an upgrade in their current employment and almost half expected to continue in a graduate program at an even higher level after they completed their current program. In education, for example, almost 70 percent were planning to continue to a Rank 1 certification in teaching; roughly 20 percent were hoping to obtain a doctoral degree; and about 10 percent were seeking a principalship. In every category reflecting satisfaction with various aspects of the program (including admissions, registration, student services, library services, computer services, and counseling services) on a five-point scale, the lowest score on a five-year mean was 3.9. In areas related to faculty competencies, the lowest score for the same time period was 4.1.[57]

Today, a total of 35 undergraduate majors, three minors, and ten pre-professional or graduate programs are available. A new center in northern Kentucky opened in the fall of 2012 to provide opportunities, especially those in the health sciences. Having known Taylor's objections years ago to extension centers, I was surprised to learn about this new center. He is excited about online courses in part because they require no new facilities to build or maintain. Cockrum explained the need for physical space in a heavily populated area: there are not enough clinics or hospitals in the Williamsburg area to provide the rotations that are required for the majors in the Physicians Assistant program or in the new Ph.D. in Clinical Psychology. Students in Williamsburg will be allowed to go to northern

Kentucky for their rotations, and eventually students will be able to take all their requirements in these majors at the new branch. The Lifelong Learning program offered there will allow degree completion in business administration, psychology, human services, and criminal justice.

Like so many I asked about what makes UC successful, Dehne responded, "Jim Taylor: President Taylor has been very thoughtful about expanding the college, incorporating the liberal arts into the programs directed toward professional fields and utilizing new techniques for offering education, such as online courses." While online courses remain less attractive than traditional in-class ones in significant ways, they do provide ways for education to be more affordable and more accessible.

Taylor insists that the driving force behind the rise of the online program at UC is Cockrum and his office. In a speech he made about new directions in higher education, Cockrum stressed the importance of a broad-based education: "I'm convinced that the broader based your education is, the more marketable you will be."[58] For those who cannot afford to relocate to a college campus, online programs provide access to credentials that make it possible for the students to excel personally and professionally. And online courses can broaden the base of education even for those students studying on a traditional college campus.

It is clear that both online and face-to-face instruction are important:

> . . . For the hundreds of less well-endowed private colleges . . . online learning is a critical tool, particularly in hybrid form. For example, a course with four face-to-face classroom sessions per week can be redesigned to have only half as many professor-led discussions, the balance being replaced with online student-to-student learning led by a skilled but less expensive adjunct instructor. The full-time professor is thus freed up to serve more students or engage in more scholarship.

> At the same time, all liberal arts colleges must preserve their advantages in memory and mentoring . . . . The instruction of the liberal arts college should remain predominantly face-to-face and its curriculum cross-disciplinary . . . where online learning is part of a "high-tech/high-touch" education.[59]

UC is working hard to find the right mix of the various methods.

(See Appendix F for a chronological listing of academic changes over the past eight years.)

Enrollments

Enrollments at the College in early years were pitifully small in comparison to the figures of today, often consisting of fewer than 100 students. The years under Boswell (1947-1980), however, saw enrollments increase from 200 to just over 2,000 by 1980, when Taylor was named president. There were often several hundred students who lived at home or in off-campus apartments and many did not attend classes full time. However, most of the students during those early years were residential undergraduates who took a full load of classes. That enrollment pattern held fairly steady until the 1980s when economic downturns, escalating energy costs and increasing competition from the community colleges and expansion of the regional state universities with branches opening across the state created growing pressure on the small private colleges, especially those in isolated regions of the country. By 1980, the baby-boomers who swelled campuses in the 1960s had graduated; and it was programs designed for adult learners, those focusing primarily on professional programs, that kept enrollments at least steady for many colleges during the decade.[60] By the 1990s, enrollments at Cumberland had dropped to around 1,300, eventually stabilizing around 1,400. The majority of the college population in America was over the age of 22; and more than 40 percent of all college students were part-timers.[61]

Much of the credit for the increases in enrollments at UC can be given to the creative staff who have stayed in touch with the communication preferences of typical high school graduates. Recruitment for these traditional, residential students heavily involves new social media such as Twitter and Facebook. For the class of 2017, the College has established a Facebook Community which encourages students planning to enroll in the fall of 2013 to meet and stay in touch with each other electronically.[62]

Like other colleges that have traditionally focused almost all recruiting on the traditional undergraduate students and most programming on the liberal arts,

Cumberland College came to recognize that the economies of the future would require that college graduates be prepared to change jobs a number of times over a lifetime—or to see the jobs they held change. To help prepare students for the competitive job market, the College, while maintaining a requirement that all students take courses in the liberal arts, became a university and started, more than ever, emphasizing the pre-professional fields. It also began to offer older students—those who had completed secondary school and perhaps even some college—programs likely to attract them to the University. As a university, the institution has explored and adopted new technologies, new teaching techniques, and new graduate offerings in the fields of education, business, and medically related fields; and enrollments have grown and are continuing to grow. Cockrum's office reports impressive enrollment figures for the University: each year since 2000, enrollment has increased by several hundred students. In 2000 the fall headcount was fewer than 2,000 students; by 2012 the total was almost 4,300.

By the late 1990s, the non-residential and non-traditional students began to outnumber the residential, traditional ones at some colleges and universities. Today most of these off-campus students are enrolled in online graduate programs, some of which are offered entirely online with some being "blended," i.e., requiring some time on campus in a classroom setting and additional work online, and some being entirely online. By fall of the 2012-2013 academic year, the count of residential students at UC was approximately 1,150 with a headcount of 1,864 students taking courses on campus either full or part-time. One interesting fact about the enrollment figures for the fall of 2012 is that there were 2,433 full time and part-time graduate students for a total headcount of 4,297 students. There can be little doubt that the College plans to continue to expand offerings available for the non-traditional college populations. When undergraduate enrollment for 2012-2013 was up approximately 8 percent from the previous fall, enrollment for online programs was up 18 percent.[63]

Most of the UC students continue to come from the Appalachian region. For the 2011-2012 year, 46 percent of those enrolled were from counties designated by the Appalachian Regional Commission as Appalachian. For the online graduate programs, 85 percent of those enrolled were from Kentucky and 15 percent were from other states and countries. As

UC expands the number of its online course offerings, more and more enrollments are expected to reflect a widening geographic area.[64]

(See Appendix G for fall enrollment figures over recent years.)

Assessment

In 2005, UC established the Center for Teaching and Learning to support faculty development and to provide curricular and co-curricular activities enhancing critical thinking and learning skills. Even years prior to the establishment of this office, the College had a system of assessment looking at general education critical thinking skills. Susan Weaver, who had spent a total of 20 years teaching sociology at Miami University and Marshall University, was inspired by the center for learning at Miami to accept responsibility for overseeing this unit at UC. In this case, coming from outside the regional culture, with no prior experience at the University, helped establish Weaver as an objective observer and gave her credibility with both local faculty and staff and evaluators from outside the College. Weaver and Fish, in his role as Associate Dean of Academic Affairs, work with assessment coordinators across the departments and the assessment committee to improve the assessment process and keep it current with SACS standards. Incoming freshmen and second semester juniors are tested every year and their scores compared. When an overall cohort score reflects a weakness, faculty and staff meet to determine how to address that concern. For example, when math scores were low at one point, several professors developed an emphasis on including math and chart-reading skills into non-math courses.[65]

Weaver gives Fish a lot of credit for the progress made in the assessment arena. He has served on multiple on-site and off-site committees for SACS, developing assessments for multiple programs in addition to the work he has done at UC helping call attention to the work that has to be done to assure continued accreditation by SACS. He has clarified expectations and updated assessment standards to the current SACS standards and developed a template for assessment audits. Weaver herself has worked with the Wabash College Center of Inquiry in the Liberal Arts and brought expertise and experience to the issue of assessment at the University.

One aspect of Weaver's work is related to experiments the University conducts to determine the best way to encourage students to take the tests and to take the tests seriously. Originally testing was done on a Saturday and on a voluntary basis; later the testing for juniors was worked into class time in individual courses; then a special time when all juniors were required to take the test was established. To improve the effort that students put into taking the test, various reward systems have been tried: candy was offered to one group taking the test; another group was offered a gift certificate if their freshmen scores improved. Plans for the future include the possibility of requiring those with low scores to take remedial work before graduation. The National Survey of Student Engagement (NSSE) has been added to measure the degree to which students participate in the learning experiences of the University.

Weaver provided a lot of general information related to how the University attempts to provide the best learning experiences possible. To respond to an interest in keeping a focus on general education requirements throughout the higher education experience, UC introduced integrated studies for juniors and seniors—classes small in size to enhance the students' abilities in writing and critical thinking. Throughout their course of study, students must meet competency requirements in writing, math and scientific reasoning, historical and cultural understanding, aesthetic appreciation and social and professional awareness. Weaver is constantly reviewing new ways of measuring these competencies for better comparisons.

In addition to standard approaches to assessing student learning, alumni are surveyed periodically; graduating seniors are surveyed each year; and other surveys help measure the success of various offices across the campus, such as the library, the registrar's office and the office of student employment. Evaluations of online courses, courses taught by adjuncts, and those taught by faculty with less than two years of experience are conducted for every class. All other faculty conduct evaluations in two classes each year with results being reviewed by chairs who can then work with the faculty to make improvements when necessary. Evaluations of online courses are maintained separately from those for in-class courses to help determine how equivalent the educational experiences are. Faculty continue to assess students in individual classes through general tests, portfolios, and special projects or presentations. Some use new tools (such as iClickers, Turning Point Technology, and polleverywhere.com) for quizzes at the beginning of each class to help identify materials to emphasize in class lectures and discussions.

While each program has an assessment coordinator, departments such as education have special reports and assessments required for accreditations, and these generally require more attention to assessment than is typical. The registrar's office handles the collection of data related to retention and graduation rates and other information required by external agencies and requested by various campus divisions. Assessment coordinators are individuals who attend assessment meetings and gather data from faculty, such as final exam scores, writing scores or other measures used for assessments. They enter data into appropriate forms and write the executive summary for that program. Some are appointed, but most are volunteers who know that assessment is a critical part of the educational process. Some departments have several such coordinators: business has separate ones for accounting, business administration, management information software (MIS), business online and the MBA program. Education has different coordinators for undergraduate, MAT, Ed.D., MA.Ed., and School Counseling. In the department of English/Modern Foreign Language, English has one and Modern Foreign Language has another. Math/physics has one for math and one for physics.

These reviews taking place across the campus on a regular basis have led to clear standards and expectations: a plan for improved assessment and feedback to department chairs to communicate clear standards about expectations for specific assessment targets, methods, and benchmarks; standardization of data and the expectations that data will be reported on a four-point scale when possible; use of benchmarks; introduction of separate reports for online programs to ensure equal expectations and assessments; and use of iLearn to provide data to programs and to permit uploading of departmental minutes and assessment reports. Generic information is housed on one website and another serves as the repository for data collected.

All of these efforts to determine what the students are learning produce reports that are shared with the General Education Committee, the University Assessment Committee and the individual departments. Departments share the minutes of their meetings when assessment is discussed so that Weaver's office can track trends and uses of assessment tools and results. Weaver also develops seminars and other programs to promote new and better tools for assessment and the use of results. Various departments have made changes as the result of information gathered; for example a course in the use of technology to teach music has been added to the curriculum to enhance the experiences of students planning to teach and/or compose. Changes that have impacted student life across the campus include those related to renovations in the dorms and wellness facilities, changes in menu choices (such as allowing students to use their meal cards at the steakhouse in the Cumberland Inn and serving less fried food in the cafeteria), and new focuses for campus missions.

Weaver's comment to me about assessment at UC reflects what I heard repeatedly across the campus: faculty, staff, and administrators are collaborative and cooperative. "Excellent communication and an administration that encourages innovation create a great campus climate that fosters growth and improvement. Campuses who share a sense of openness can benefit from the approach that we use of collaborating rather than issuing ultimatums about assessment."[66]

Graduates

A board report for June, 2012, indicates that in the past the major focus of the College was on recruitment and enrollment, but today the emphasis on retention and graduation is just as strong. The retention rate between freshman and sophomore years is 62 percent while the average for all private colleges in the region is 59 percent. The graduation rate over five years is 43 percent, versus an average rate of 39 percent across the colleges.[67]

One of the most significant research studies undertaken by the ACA was the one on alumni conducted by Ernest Pascarella and Patrick Terenzini. That study was based on a survey of roughly 47,000 alumni who had graduated from colleges in the ACA and selected public universities in the region 5, 15, and 25 years before. According to George Kuh, best known for his research on assessing the student and institutional performances that enhance success in the undergraduate experience, "The study is particularly rich in that the researchers were able to link pre-college data from an ACT assessment done at the time of college matriculation to a variety of college outcomes. This allows for controlling for salient factors, such as high school grades, parents' income and educational attainment, and institutional selectivity." On most measures, the graduates of the private colleges performed at levels 10 to 34 percent higher than those from the comprehensive public universities: "developing ethical standards and values, appreciating literature and fine arts, developing self-confidence, actively participating in volunteer work to support worthwhile causes, interacting well with people from racial groups or cultures different from their own, and learning how to be a more responsible family member." The overall satisfaction with the undergraduate education received was 10.7 percent higher for the graduate of the private colleges. The graduates of the public colleges showed more use of technology (4.1 percent); more reading of newspapers (2.9 percent); more watching of information programs on television (3.9 percent); and a salary advantage (3.2 percent).[68] Given the focus of the private colleges on service and the high employment rates in the non-profit sector of their graduates, this salary advantage was not unexpected.

The University maintains an office for career services to assist those expecting to graduate from the institution. Debbie Harp, another graduate of Cumberland College and long-time employee there, answers to the vice-president for Student Services, but she is the sole employee of the office helping with career planning. She serves a variety of responsibilities, including conducting interest inventories and advising students about career options for lower classmen and helping juniors and seniors prepare resumes and cover letters. She facilitates the University's work with a regional job market and holds similar events on the campus. Currently, the surveys for graduates and alumni do not ask the questions that would allow for the compilation of data regarding percentages of students who find jobs in their fields or get admitted to graduate programs, but that data will be collected when future funding is available for hiring additional staff. Harp helps students find internships, especially those studying in the Hutton business school, and she has a number of internships available in health fields and at local businesses, such as Wal mart. She also provides programs on issues such as substance abuse and sexual assault; and she coordinates the mental health services with outside agencies and consultants to provide help to students in need of assistance. Both on-campus and online students can access the services of Harp's office, but the vast majority of the over one thousand contacts made each year are from residential students. Evaluations of services provided indicate a satisfaction rate for the services of roughly 4.0 on a five-point scale.[69]

Security

The University considers safety and security an important part of the culture of the campus. The local police in Williamsburg have the same authority on the campus as they do across the city, and the University outsources security services for 24/7 patrol of the campus. It seems that crime is minimal on the campus; most episodes occur at the end of a semester when a student decides he or she wants something on the campus that belongs to someone else. Reports of physical violence are rare, and students say they feel safe on the campus.

It can be argued that crime in the 1990s was significantly less serious a problem on college campuses than it is today, but one of my favorite Cumberland College stories is about a crime that occurred on the campus in that decade: two boys from "out in the country" decided to come to the campus and break into the science building to steal a few computers. After taking the computers, their truck would not start so they asked a maintenance man if he could loan them jumper cables. The maintenance man realized what was happening and called the police to arrest the boys. This story reflects at least one of the reasons that the students say they feel secure on the campus: maintenance staff as well as security officers are prepared to protect them.

A more recent incident in 2010 reflects a situation virtually every campus I know has faced at some level: drugs on campus. The administrators at UC are unwilling to tolerate any level of such abuse once they are alerted to it. A prime example occurred when accusations were made, and the University installed hidden cameras that videotaped three students smoking marijuana. The students involved were not simply brought before a campus disciplinary board; the University contacted the Williamsburg Police Department and Operation UNITE (an acronym for Unlawful Narcotics Investigations, Treatment and Education), and the suspected parties were arrested. UNITE strives to eliminate the use of illegal drugs in eastern Kentucky by working with local and federal drug enforcement agencies, coordinating treatment for users, supporting families and friends of such abusers, and providing educational experiences for the public about the dangers of using such drugs. Perhaps the serious problem the region has with drug abuse intensifies the emphasis on the prevention that the University takes; the rules are strict and enforced rigorously. Taylor explained the arrest situation to the trustees: **"We tell them [students] about the rules before they ever come to campus as students . . . . Our goal is to make students whole in competence and in character. While we believe in forgiveness, reconciliation and restoration, we also believe in responsibility for one's actions, and we believe in accountability."**[70]

With a team of contracted security officers on campus 24/7, the Williamsburg Police Department patrolling the campus at various times, the Whitley County 911 dispatch service always available, security cameras at major buildings and an emergency notification system, students at UC should feel secure anywhere anytime on the campus. For freshmen and others who choose to attend, the Student Services office offers seminars on topics such as Sexual Assault and Dating Violence Prevention and Alcohol Abuse Prevention. Students who violate the institution's alcohol policy are required to attend a special session about the dangers of alcohol. The Campus Crime Report that every college is required by law to maintain indicates that in 2011 that there were only 34 crimes against campus property and 19 in residential facilities. For a campus housing well over 1000 students, 53 incidents considered criminal in one year's time does not seem shocking, and those "crimes" were ones of theft or burglary, alcohol abuse, menacing behaviors with a total of three sexual offenses—not manslaughter or even possession of weapons. As one student who remains anonymous reported, "Security is always available, dorms are locked and secured at regular times, the campus is well lighted. I have no concerns about safety on this campus."

Taylor admits that being next to a major interstate is both a blessing and a curse: the traffic carries both potential students and donors and some the University would prefer not visit the area. But with its location in a region known largely for the feuding of the Hatfields and McCoys and the corrupt sheriff in the *Dukes of Hazard*, the University property itself might be described as an island of safety in a sea of danger.

Athletics

Although athletics at UC is not "the face of the university" as it is at some major universities, the University has increasingly come to value having a variety of athletic teams; Randy Vernon, who coached the basket team from 1979 until 2000, spoke about being the first athletic director to serve in the position full-time—a distinction that is the result of the growth in emphasis on athletics across the campus. When Vernon came to the College as the basketball coach, there were eight athletic teams. Today there are 22 different teams (11 for men and 11 for women): baseball, basketball, cross country, football, golf, soccer, swimming, tennis, track and field, and wrestling for men; and basketball, cross country, golf, soccer, softball, swimming, tennis, track and field, volleyball, and wrestling for women. UC also offers co-ed cheerleading and archery. Plans are in the works for adding lacrosse and bowling. And plans for renovating new land recently purchased by the University include adding new athletic fields.

Both on the field and on the court, the Patriots have claimed recognition. Over the past 18 years, they have won the All-Sports Conference President's Cup, a measure of excellence across all the sports in conference competition, 12 times; until recent years they had won it more than all the other colleges combined, and recently they have maintained a ranking as second or third. For the 2011 year, UC tied for first place in the competition of the six fall sports. In the NAIA conference, they are usually in the top 25 among approximately 300 schools listed.

The University places a high value on maintaining a strong reputation not only for having winning teams, but also for having athletes who strive to be good students and good citizens. Students can get assistance in the Academic Resource Center (ARC), a tutoring center for all students, and each coach maintains study halls that are not required by the institution. In the past 13 years, UC students have won 24 of 34 awards given by the Mid-South Conference to recognize Scholar Athletes—12 in the men's and 12 in the women's divisions. They are noted not only for maintaining high rankings in athletic events but also for volunteering with Mountain Outreach and other campus service projects. And retention rates for the athletes are roughly the same as those for all UC undergraduates.[71]

While offering a variety of athletic teams is an important part of the effort to recruit students, learning to play as a team member and serving as a responsible representative of the University at various events off the campus provide an important part of the education student-athletes receive. At many institutions of higher education, athletics define the college or university. At UC athletics are a very important part of the institutional culture and a critical part of the higher education experience for many students, but the athletic teams and events do not determine the direction the University takes or the priorities of the moment. They are simply part of an overall emphasis on the growth and maturity of the students. Equally important aspects are the work and service programs with the academic programs being the critical element in every student's experience.

Work Program

When I was working at the ACA in a building on the Berea College campus, I was fascinated by what are known as the work colleges—seven colleges across the US where every student attending is required to work from 10 to 20 hours beyond that expected from courses taken. These colleges draw significant federal dollars to support their work programs—the largest estimated as receiving over a million dollars each year. I could not understand why more colleges did not become work colleges. Then I learned why: requiring every student to work a set number of hours each week is difficult when some have very heavy class schedules and they participate on athletic teams and in service and social clubs. Also, students can often make more money working at sites off the campus. Finally, each college is required to maintain an administrative office for the work program that is comparable to the one maintained for the academic program—and operating an administrative office is expensive. One of the current work colleges has even expressed concerns about enrollment growth; the fear is that if enrollment increases significantly, it will be difficult to provide meaningful jobs for all of the students. I have come to understand that programs similar to the one at Cumberland, where students have the opportunity to work but not the obligation, might be more efficient and just as effective in helping students appreciate the value of and joy in work.

Through a variety of "workships" students at UC can receive compensation for labor assignments across the campus—doing general office work, maintenance, construction, and other assignments that help instill the importance of labor and provide experiences which can enhance their education and prepare them for the world of work. Some funding comes from a federal work-study program open to all colleges and universities, but in many cases UC has to raise the money to employ students; as a result, not every student is able to work as many hours as he or she would like. Students can request and are selected for work assignments based on criteria related to needs of the institution and abilities of the students. In a typical semester, roughly 800 students work an average of 11.5 hours each week.[72]

In 2010, UC hired its first dean of student employment to identify and publicize various positions and job descriptions and to train and maintain communications with those who supervise the student labor force to assure that all are in compliance with federal policies governing student labor. Peggy Woods, like so many of her colleagues in the administration of the University, graduated from Cumberland College and took a position away from the region; her employment was in the Kentucky Cabinet for Health and Human Services. From there, she became a training specialist for a major university in the state before returning to her native Whitley County to work for UC. She takes great pride in the fact that so many UC students have the chance to work to cover part of their expenses as well as to learn "the value of promptness, industry, dependability and initiative."[73]

Woods explained that one reason this student employment office is separate from the general personnel office of the University is to provide the support that allows students to select jobs they want instead of simply having jobs assigned to them without necessarily any consideration for their personal aspirations. The new staff works with students to schedule their workships around their co-curricular activities and classes as well as to help them gain experience in the fields they may want to consider as majors—though in some cases the needs of the University have to come before those of the students so some do not get placements they consider particularly relevant to their futures. Currently, there are about 800 student employees working under federal funding or institutional funding. Serious efforts are made to allow every student to work at least 10 hours a week. Through these jobs, students learn what it means to have a boss who can hire you, discipline you, and fire you if your efforts do not match his or her expectations. While UC does not maintain transcripts for the students reflecting their success in their work experiences separate from their regular academic transcripts, the University does maintain records of the various positions each student holds during the years at UC, and some students hold a different job each semester. The office provides manuals for both students and supervisors to help with training and disciplinary procedures.[74]

Community Outreach

Presidents of small colleges are frequently asked to serve on the boards of various community organizations. Over the years, Taylor has held a number of such positions with various civic and non-profit organizations, including the Mid-Appalachia College Television Council, Bell-Whitley Community Service Agency, Rotary Club, Masonic Lodge #490, and Cumberland River District Mental Health-Mental Retardation Board. He has also served on boards of several for-profit organizations in the community, including the Bank of Williamsburg and Forcht Bank, a bank started by a former UC faculty member. He has chaired 35 reaffirmation of accreditation visits for SACS; served two terms on the Executive Committee of SACS; served two terms on the Appeals Committee of SACS; chaired the Mid-South Athletic Conference; chaired the Association of Christian Colleges and Universities; chaired the Southern Baptist College Association and served on the ACA board since its inception, including multiple terms as an officer. His volunteer work is limited by the time he spends traveling for the University, but perhaps the University programs he supports the most strongly outside those related to the academic departments are those that serve communities beyond the borders of the campus.[75]

The president of neighboring Alice Lloyd College recently commented on the graduates from Cumberland as well as those from Alice Lloyd: "These types of schools—Alice Lloyd, Cumberland, Berea—help build character at a time when it seems the world of higher education is getting away from that goal. When the graduates get ready to find a job, there is something to be said for their having been at a character-based institution."[76] There are not so many places today where a student can get an education at the same time there is a focus on building his or her character. A major part of the character building that takes place at UC happens through its various community service projects.

Students on the campus have for decades recognized how blessed they are to live in modern, comfortable housing and have abundant food and other necessities—in part because most come from depressed areas or they see in Whitley County as soon as they leave the campus how poverty can destroy motivation and create conditions that jeopardize health as well as happiness. Over the years, the College has developed a number of programs designed to encourage the students to help those less fortunate—all the while realizing that people living in poverty can become accepting of their plight and become part of the problem rather than part of the solution.

In addition to the academic transcript, the University maintains a Service Leadership Transcript for every student, reflecting the formal activities the student has participated in outside the classroom during his or her years at UC. In 2011-2012 the UC students contributed a total of 45,832 hours of community service; 88 percent of the graduates for the year exceeded the required 40 hours of service. Over 85 percent of the graduating students agreed their commitment to helping others was stronger after the UC experiences, and almost 75 percent said they had assumed a leadership role in some aspect of the campus life, especially through their service experiences. The hours that students document were spent in community service are all reviewed by members of the administration to ensure that the student services were meaningful and valued by the community organizations. Surveys of both graduating students and alumni indicate that the community service focus of the University has made them more aware of the problems and challenges all communities face.[77]

Appalachian Ministries

Appalachian Ministries is a program established in 1975 that works with local youth in the community, taking them to various churches and programs in the area for recreation and instructional programs. Participating students also hold food drives; visit nursing homes; and volunteer at recycling centers and emergency shelters.

Baptist Campus Ministries

The Baptist Campus Ministries is a student group led by an upperclassman that plans campus-wide fellowship and renewal events with guest speakers on campus and takes teams of students to witness and assist in local nursing homes and other such service organizations. On occasion they travel to other cities and states to assist groups from ministries at other colleges with service in areas of critical need.

Mountain Outreach

The best known of the campus service programs is one started by students over 30 years ago, and ably led today by Marc Hensley, who entered the College as a student shortly after high school but left to marry and raise a family. After holding a variety of jobs, he returned to the College as a non-traditional student and completed his degree in 2005. In 2006 he became the director of Mountain Outreach and continued his education to receive an MA at UC. The sad state of many of the homes in the region is reflected by what I witnessed while visiting: property the University had recently purchased included a number of very dilapidated homes, but many of those moving out of the homes scheduled for demolition were capturing every part of the houses they could carry with them—including siding they were tearing from the outside walls.

A campus brochure describes the moving story of the development of Mountain Outreach. In the early 1980s some students not from the region were horrified by what they saw when driving around the Williamsburg community—how ramshackle many of the homes were; some had neither electricity nor running water. Two of those students tried to repair one of the homes, but quickly realized the need for a new house. In 1982, the students began Mountain Outreach by recruiting 20 other students to build a house for a man and his handicapped son living in a shack that was beyond repair. The boys found a building site—though there was no road to it and no electricity nearby. Using hand-operated tools and carrying lumber and other supplies by hand to the site, they built this first house by begging or borrowing equipment and supplies from local businesses and recruiting additional volunteers from among the skilled contractors, electricians and plumbers in the town. Unfortunately, the man who had inspired the students to take on a task for which they had no preparation died before the house was finished. The boys, however, went on to oversee the building of nine houses and repairs on numerous others before they graduated in 1984.

Mountain Outreach continues through the commitment of the College and the hard work of hundreds of students and other volunteers. Since 1982, 141 new houses have been built and given to local families selected by students from applications made by those in need. The recipients of the homes are obligated to make small monthly payments to cover the cost of materials; labor is donated by students and various other groups, primarily ones from churches around the region. The total number of homes built in a typical year is three and the number repaired is often 30 or more.

Mountain Outreach also hosts programs for those living in the houses built, including ones on managing finances. When a family is identified by the students to receive one of the newly built homes, the University provides the financing which the family will need—generally about $50,000. Then to help assure the family maintains the low monthly repayments, UC sometimes provides consulting and programs related to money management. Also, the Mountain Outreach staff maintain a food pantry and a clothing store for needy families and a Christmas center which prepares gifts for children in the region.

A 2012 brochure lists several honors that have recognized the contributions of Mountain Outreach: the Acton Institute for the Study of Religion and Liberty selected it to receive one of ten Samaritan Awards; *USA Today* noted it in the 1996 "Make a Difference Day" competition; and President George H. Bush recognized the program as his 220th Point of Light.

The benefits to the students of working with Mountain Outreach go well beyond those of many service projects. They learn construction skills, sometimes including plumbing and wiring, and they learn how to run programs for identifying recipients of the houses and for helping the new occupants build their financial futures. What remains most important, however, is the sense of responsibility and pride they develop by helping others climb out of poverty.

Hutton Leadership Program

Leadership training is an integral part of campus life with students attending leadership seminars during the time they are involved in a service activity. The seminars provide students with the opportunity to learn how to organize and lead others as well as to grow in awareness of their responsibilities to others. The Service Leadership Transcripts maintained by the University to document formal service and similar activities outside the classroom indicate that over 33 percent of the students document over 200 hours of service before graduation. Such students are named Hutton Scholars. In terms of value to the community, statistics suggest that in the 15 years of the program, the monetary contribution (based on minimum wage) of the work provided in the community by UC students is almost $4 million dollars.[78]

Other Contributions

The University hosts a variety of programs for the community, such as wellness fairs (offering free cholesterol, glucose and blood pressure screening) and celebrations on July 4 and September 11 each year at the campus Patriot Park. It provides free use (including set-up and clean-up) of the football stadium for all-star games and free use of the track for public school events and general exercise. Other facilities are available for free for the Kiwanis Club, the Southeastern Kentucky Chamber of Commerce, the Whitley County Genealogical Society, and drug and alcohol prevention programs. Training provided the Williamsburg Police Department is offered on the campus, and uniformed police officers are invited to eat free in the campus dining hall. UC has provided contributions toward equipment for the police and has helped purchase a fire truck for the city.[79] Over the past two years, the University has hosted an event for fifth-grade students across surrounding counties; the students came to the campus for a day's study of the history of the Revolutionary Period, and they were given name tags that enable them to attend campus programs (including athletic events and concerts) for free so long as they are students in a public school system; the local chapter of the Sons of the American Revolution and the National Guard assisted with the presentations. Once a year, the University hosts an event to honor local heroes from the town and county.

Physical Plant

One thing I have repeatedly been struck by is how clean most of the campuses of the ACA colleges are; even the most dilapidated dormitory will often have fresh paint on the walls and scrubbed floors. But at UC, it is not just that the buildings and grounds are clean; there appears to be little, if any, deferred maintenance at any of the buildings or grounds or sports areas. The University maintains a schedule of repairs that stays ahead of tangible indications that it is time for repair of a building or trimming of shrubs. When a new roof is added, the budgets anticipate the need for another new one in roughly 20 years. There are none of the types of buildings that I frequently saw on my visits to the campuses of ACA colleges: buildings that looked deserted, ones that were explained as being "for storage."

The original building of the Williamsburg Institute,[80] Roburn Hall, was built in 1888 at a cost of $12,000. At that time, it was known as the classroom building for the 200 students enrolled. Today, it is a dorm, housing 38 students. By 1907, three other buildings and the president's house had been added, though the president's house was not given to the College until the Boswell presidency. When Taylor was head of development for the College, some of his major priorities were the building of Boswell Campus Center, Asher Hall (dormitory) and the McGaw Music Building. Once he became president, he immediately focused on "improving store front appeal" by removing over 300 dying trees and demolishing over 50 dilapidated houses.[81] Other buildings were added: O. Wayne Rollins Center, the Cumberland Inn and Conference Center, the Jim Taylor II Stadium, Siler Hall and Kleist Hall (both dormitories for men). Since 2000 the list of new buildings has included the Grace Crum Rollins Fine Arts

Center, Hutton Hall and Harth Hall (both residences for women), the Hutton School of Business, an extension to the Correll Science Complex and a number of fields and courts that accommodate the growing number of athletic teams.

One retired administrator talked about traveling with Taylor: during such trips, when they passed near a college campus, the two would stop to look at facilities and take pictures of features they thought could be incorporated into the Cumberland College campus.[82] Over the 20 years between 1972 and 2002, the College added 20 new buildings and renovated 12. Kyle Gilbert, Vice President of Operations, reports that today the main campus includes 110 acres and 32 buildings, with a new health and wellness center being added to the recently remodeled Student Center.[83] In one semester, the fall of 2009, the University dedicated the Ward and Regina Correll Science Complex, the Terry and Marion Forcht Medical Wing, the Clyde Faulkner Business Classroom, the E.S. Moss-Roburn Hall Building.[84] New housing is being planned for students in the graduate health fields; this housing will be in the form of apartments so that if the space is ever not needed for students, it can be rented to faculty or to people from outside the University.

The building some have felt ambivalent about is the Cumberland Inn and Conference Center. When the inn was being built, President Taylor said that he thought the greatest form of flattery was duplication, and he had always admired Boone Tavern, the inn of Berea College, so he was constructing a similar building. When I told John Stephenson, the president at Berea College at that time, Taylor's remark, Stephenson's response was, "He should have told me; I would have given him ours." In both cases (though built almost one hundred years apart), the buildings were intended to provide lodging and meals for visitors to the campus and region. And in both cases, they have provided labor assignments for students from the campuses and visibility for the colleges, but both inns have also created financial stress for the college budgets. Taylor reflects on the financial deficit that the Cumberland Inn shows in some years, but he still considers it a good investment for the visibility it provides the University, the jobs it provides for students, and the relationships it fosters with donors. Dehne sees the building of the Cumberland Inn as "a masterful move to attract attention and people to the College."[85] (See Appendix H for a listing of buildings and facilities.)

UC also owns 13,000 acres of land that are not a part of the 110 acres of the main campus. Of that total, 8,700 acres is undeveloped land that was given to the College in the early part of the twentieth century. Heirs of Henry Clay Frick had given the land to be shared by Princeton, Harvard and MIT. A logical assumption is that Frick's family gave the land with the expectation that use of the land would in some way benefit Appalachia, where Frick had collected some of the coal resources that enabled him to develop one of the largest steel companies in the world. In 1933, those colleges deeded the property to Cumberland College (perhaps thinking that was a way to help Appalachia) but retained the oil and gas and some mineral rights.[86] In 2009, the University asked that those rights revert to UC; having the rights would save some $300,000 per year for natural gas, provide well over $100,000 income and increase the options for use of the land. While the estimated value of the property is almost $17 million, its value is limited without title to the oil and gas rights.[87] The biology program uses some sites on the land for environmental monitoring and research, but more extensive use would be facilitated by having control of all the natural resources of the property. In 2009, I worked with the University to contact several people connected to Princeton to ask if that university would consider some arrangement whereby UC could gain control of the rights Princeton and the other institutions continue to hold related to the property. In December of 2009,

Taylor received a brief note from a lawyer at Princeton indicating that the universities owning the rights were not prepared to consider donating those rights to Cumberland College at that time.

Under the capable direction of Gilbert, a graduate of the College who has a background in architectural engineering and whose father once served in the same role as Vice President for Operations, the institution has continued to expand its main campus and recently purchased 35 acres and 65 small, dilapidated houses that will be torn down to extend the grounds of the University closer to the interstate and increase the numbers of athletic fields available. Taylor feels he has at least made major steps toward building the campus he dreamed: **"We've attacked the building of the university and the expansion of its footprint with the quote from the Bishop of Seville in the back of our mind: 'Let us build such a monumental and beautiful campus that those who come after us may think us mad to have attempted it.'"**[88]

In 1983, when I first started work at the ACA, I listened to faculty at Cumberland complain about the money and time the president was pouring into the physical plant and grounds. Today there seem to be few, if any, complaints; I never heard any during this study of the campus. In fact, one professor pointed out that when parents bring their children to the campus during recruiting events, in nine of ten cases, the first thing a parent will say is, "You certainly have a beautiful campus." Today it is one aspect of the campus that everyone seems most proud to display. **"To many who walk this campus, it is everything one imagines a university should look like . . . rolling hills, spiraling cupolas and steeples, bell-towers, uniform red brick Georgian style buildings, manicured lawns and shrubs."**[89]

CHAPTER 5: FUTURE GOALS

In 1995, the goals for the University were "reducing debt, increasing compensation, increasing endowment, increasing the level of institutional effectiveness."[1] Today the institution has those same goals, but it seems even more aware of its responsibility to the past. As the Strategic Plan for 2020 says, "A school should honor its traditions and culture and seek to move forward with those in mind."[2]

In recent years, UC has focused heavily on creating an attractive and comfortable campus as well as providing a broad-based curriculum of graduate courses and online programs. It has not lost sight of the needs of students for financial assistance or of the importance of providing a strong background in the liberal arts and measuring learning outcomes. The primary goal of the University has remained providing access to a quality education for financially disadvantaged students, not increasing its standing in national polls or increasing enrollments by developing amenities that include a growing number of recreational facilities or living accommodations that focus primarily on giving the students a luxurious lifestyle or increasing income by offering quick degrees with minimum content.

When UC compares its data with a list of indicators reflecting that a college is in trouble, the University scores reflect concerns and strengths. Tuition discounting of more than 35 percent is a sign a college is stressed, and UC's is 42 percent; more than 10 percent of the operating budget should be dedicated to technology, but UC only dedicates 3.1 percent; more than 20 percent of alumni should give annually, but only 17 percent of the UC alumni give.[3] While UC is working toward increasing funding for technology and improving the percentage of alumni giving, the other area that the data would suggest needs attention is tuition discounting.

However, the University does not discount just to attract more students; discounting at UC is for the purpose of achieving its major goal: helping as many deserving disadvantaged students as possible.

The University can be comforted by other indicators suggesting the institution is strong. According to one study about such indicators, debt service should not be more than 10 percent of annual operating budget, and UC's is 5.22 percent. Tuition dependency should be less than 85 percent; UC's is 64.8 percent. The average alumni gift should be more than $75; although not many alumni give, the average gift for the last few years at UC has been over $500. A college with an enrollment of fewer than 1,000 students is seriously endangered, but Cumberland's enrollment is well over that mark. Other indicators of the University's strength include the fact that the institution has had no problem with regional accreditors; most of the faculty hold terminal degrees and are younger than 58; the University is rapidly developing complete online programs and new degree programs; and the governance and curriculum systems can approve new degree programs in a year or less (if regional and state accreditors act quickly).[4] And UC has already succeeded in achieving many of the top indicators of success listed by presidents in national interviews: a balanced budget, a strong reputation, a vision for the future that is shared across the institution, improved retention and graduation rates, a productive working relationship with the board, fund-raising goals that are typically reached, an education program that is steadily improving, and good faculty and staff morale.[5]

One concern those who care about the University have is who—or at least what kind of person—should replace President Taylor when he retires (or dies). But this concern does not seem to be an immediate one. First, Taylor does not seem to have plans to retire. He once told me, "If I am ever not the president of this institution, I don't want anyone to tell me." UC is clearly a very important part of his life; it is his legacy. Obviously, the next president can be neither weak nor lazy, and he or she must recognize what good stewards and guardians of the institution those who have led it in the past have been. The hope is that the next generation of leaders will be as hard working and dedicated as the current one, but even college leaders generally considered dedicated hard workers are awed by Taylor's energy and accomplishments.

Despite predictions that costs for higher education are not going to decline and there are no promises of economic prosperity for the future, many continue to insist, ". . . Colleges will find ways to absorb the changes, adapting as necessary, and . . . higher education will continue to be a vital enterprise for the millions of citizens who depend on it."[6] The question remaining is what shape higher education will take as it continues "to be a vital enterprise." Will online courses even at the small, private colleges become more prevalent than those held in traditional classrooms? Will some new model be formed that cannot be imagined today? UC will clearly be examining new models that appear, but the focus for the University is expected to remain on providing financially poor students with opportunities to increase strength through affirmation of their beliefs and the development of new skills and knowledge through learning, labor and service.

Despite such suggestions as those made by Astin and Lee in the 1970s and others (including President Taylor) have made since that states should provide funding for private colleges and there should be more collaboration between the public and private universities, it seems UC recognizes that it must create its own path to the future. No one in Kentucky has been more vocal than President Taylor about the cost the Commonwealth incurs each year for educating relatively wealthy students in its major universities. But after many years of preaching the value of state support for private colleges, Taylor realizes that it is highly unlikely those in charge will recognize the benefits of putting significant money into scholarships for students to attend the private colleges or universities instead of adding more buildings and bureaucracies at the public ones.

The goals expressed in the 2020 Strategic Plan indicate the University will continue to maintain a strong residential program for somewhere between 1,500 and 2,000 undergraduates and continue to build its graduate and off-campus programs. As the community colleges have grown and expanded their programs, UC has continued the approach initially taken when those two-year schools appeared in the region to compete with the four-year private colleges: expanded recruitment efforts to attract students who are prepared to compete in the four-year college arena with little or no need for remedial courses. At the same time, UC has developed articulation agreements with the nearby community and technical colleges. While the focus of the University in recruiting students remains on providing opportunities for Appalachian students of limited financial means, as the University becomes more visible nationally through its online courses and extension centers, the enrollment of both undergraduates and graduate students is expected to become less centered on eastern Kentucky and more geographically diverse.

As new students recruited are more familiar with technology and better prepared academically, advising, recreation and social experiences will be upgraded as will content offered in the various courses, and new ways of offering degrees will continue to appear. As the quality and diversity of the student body continue to increase, the University will continue efforts to hire highly talented faculty, as reflected by credentials, but it will not lose its focus on the importance of the cultural match between the faculty and institution. Departmental reviews will continue so that the University can monitor the ebb and flow of students in the various majors. Analysis and evaluation of the success of departments in recruiting new students and graduating current ones will indicate when a department needs to be closed or restructured and when new courses and departments need to be developed. The University will continue to pay attention to the demands of the market as it builds its curriculum to address those, but it will not lose sight of the value of the liberal arts.

Faculty can expect that the University will continue to strive to upgrade salaries and benefit packages to keep them competitive not only with those of the colleges in the immediate vicinity but also with those across the state and nearby regions. The University will also continue to encourage faculty to seek out opportunities for professional development and scholarly activities through grants available from the ACA and other funding agencies, such as the National Science Foundation. The faculty and staff evaluation systems will continue to be upgraded so that the University can do an increasingly better job of rewarding excellence in teaching and service.

As anyone who has been on the UC campus recently recognizes, President Taylor has a grand vision for the buildings and grounds; it is not likely that the University will pay less attention to facilities in coming years under his leadership. The trustees and administrators continue to plan new buildings with multiple uses possible for each addition. All resources will continue to be carefully managed, and the University will continue to address maintenance issues as they become apparent and to evaluate ways technology and other resources can enhance learning experiences.

It is hard to imagine how the University might improve its fund-raising efforts given the energy and salesmanship of the president. However, the current president is aware that the University needs to develop better ways of promoting its unique attributes so that more people will develop an interest in investing in it. With graduates continuing to find employment in non-profit agencies and/or companies with low wages, the University is likely to have to continue to depend heavily on increasing the endowment (currently at just over $68 million) and funding other projects under development with contributions from those who know the region or learn about it through the letters and other communications distributed by the University. Increasing the visibility of the valuable services and benefits the University provides will be critical to sustaining the institutional development program into future years when Taylor may not be able to continue his long hours of soliciting support.[7]

There are suggestions other than those already mentioned that faculty and staff and students have for the future of the University: do a better job of recognizing the responsibility the University has for the preservation of the land that it holds, develop more institutional traditions that students can identify with and claim the kind of pride in being a Patriot that UK students claim in being a Wildcat, and serve more fish in the cafeteria. Certainly all of these concerns are ones reflecting national concerns about environmental and health issues, but the one holding the most potential for the University seems to me to be that related to the environment. With over 10,000 acres of undeveloped land, UC has the potential for playing a major role in efforts to protect the environment as well as to reap benefits from the natural resources. Through such efforts the University could draw national attention to the campus in a positive way.

While UC does not offer much more in its curriculum than many small colleges or universities, its educational opportunities are a bit more creative and adventuresome and a bit less expensive than those at many small, private liberal arts colleges with only a small endowment. Its faculty are a bit warmer and more dedicated to the individuals in their classes than many in other universities, especially the large public institutions. Its students may be less prepared than many for entering the world of higher education, but they come with an inquisitive nature and are provided with an environment that both protects and challenges them. With assets like these, the future for the University promises continued growth and economic stability. With more growth and stability should come more visibility and the promise of future leadership that will continue to build this "Bright Shining City Set on a Hill."

After having been in office 27 years, Taylor was invited to talk at a national meeting about advice he would give beginning presidents. He started with warnings:

Friends may come and go but enemies collect; in fact, your former enemies can be made into friends—sometimes.

Almost every decision you make wins a friend and an enemy with the latter having a longer memory than the former.

The lion and the lamb may lie down together but the lamb won't get much sleep.

Successful institutions generate a degree of envy and hostility.

Some professors may seem to have majored in cynicism and minored in sarcasm.

Faculty morale is always at an all-time low.

It's the early worm which gets eaten.

Budgeting is an exercise in mutual dissatisfaction.

Boards of trustees have never been known to punish themselves; they have presidents to praise in good times and on whom to cast blame in bad times. Maybe that is in part why presidential tenures have not, in general, been lengthy.

Alice W. Brown

Then he moved to more positive reflections:

> **Plant ideas with the faculty so they can bubble up and you can be surprised as much as parents are to see all the beautifully wrapped presents Santa has left for the children . . . .**

> **Show humility and don't try to be the bride at every wedding or the corpse at every funeral. Recognize others' contributions.**

> **I've never known of a President . . . fired for raising too much money.**

> **Under promise and over deliver in the midst of all the ironies, paradoxes, and contradictions.**

> **At times it is better to seek forgiveness than permissions.**

> **Every college or university has a ghost or two floating around, such as former presidents in long, flowing robes, with whom you will never measure up in stature. Praise [such people] . . . .**

> **If you survive long enough, your enemies will pass on and you will move from being a politician to being a statesman.**

> **You must stay positive and optimistic—above the fray.**[8]

More recently, Taylor has concluded his advice to new presidents by saying, **"Always do what is in the best interest of your institution without giving sway to presidential whims or thoughts of legacy."**[9] It is reasonable to expect that Taylor will continue to follow his own advice as he leads the University of the Cumberlands through another decade of successful ventures.

CONCLUSIONS

When I read through the chapters in this book, I realize that UC often appears "too good to be true." Visitors to the campus have been heard to comment, "This is the way college used to be: beautiful, well-maintained buildings and grounds; caring, capable faculty; administrators who manage frugally and compassionately; a bright, energetic president willing to dedicate his life to assuring a solid future for the institution; and students who study hard and work hard to serve those in need. Still, the University sits under the shadow of gloomy predictions for colleges like itself—those religiously affiliated, located in rural areas, and holding small endowments. To address some of the dangers predicted to be ahead for many small, private colleges or universities, UC is working to increase the amount of its current endowment of roughly $70 million to $100 million. UC seems highly unlikely to change or deny its religious affiliation or change its central location to capture new populations of students, but it continues to explore online programs and new courses and degrees that might be added to the curriculum.

In the book about "invisible colleges," primarily those that are church related and have enrollments of fewer than 2,500 on-campus students, the authors compare students attending elite private colleges and those attending four-year public universities with those attending the lesser known, less competitive colleges. What they conclude is that there are major differences between the students at elite colleges and those at the invisible ones in demographics, family backgrounds, achievements in high school, and choices of careers. But the students at colleges like UC are "remarkably similar to those at the state institutions." Predictions in that book are being realized today: "The implication here is that further expansion of the public colleges will seriously hurt the invisible colleges. Moreover, as programs in nursing and the health professions are further developed in the community colleges, the invisible colleges may find themselves in competition with this group of institutions as well."[1] For the past forty years since that prediction, the public universities have continued to build extension centers close to small, private colleges, and community colleges have continued to offer programs in the health sciences, in biotechnology fields, and in many other fields where students once expected to have to attend a four-year school to acquire relevant credentials. Students who leave UC before graduating have the option of moving to a nearby state university (such as Eastern Kentucky University or Morehead State University) or to one of the local community colleges, where tuition and time to degree completion may be lower than at local private colleges. Such are some of the threats that the small, private four-year colleges have been facing and expect to continue to have to face.

A recent report lists the complaints often heard about colleges of today: ". . . students who don't learn; faculty who don't teach; escalating prices; the misplaced emphasis on rankings; out-of-control college sports; enormous sums being spent on amenities to attract students; more money going to merit as opposed to need-based student financial aid; and colleges and universities that were getting better and better at 'doing it on the cheap' to preserve their bottom line."[2] I hope this book has shown that there are still colleges where students are learning—and not just in the classroom; where teachers are teaching—and mentoring students; where at approximately $10,000 per year, the tuition remains significantly lower than that at many of the elite private colleges charging over $40,000 per year; where national rankings of colleges are not of great relevance; where athletics are highly important but not prohibitively expensive; where amenities are basically shuttle buses to large cities; where money going to students is based on need more than on merit; and where "doing it on the cheap" only means that costs in the region are generally low.

When I read national publications about the need for colleges to reduce costs, I think about how "lean and mean" operations at Cumberland College have been in the past and how UC expects to continue to operate frugally to thrive in the future. When I attend national conferences about the importance of "intentional teaching" so that students learn more than simply academic content, I think about all the efforts of the faculty at Cumberland to involve students in various approaches to learning and about the fact that Cumberland College students have always been able to learn to lead through holding responsible jobs on the campus and to develop empathy and understanding by providing services throughout the local community. When agencies of the federal government talk about the need to monitor and document the progress students make during college, I think about the exceptionally thorough evaluation and assessment processes in place at UC. When I hear about the importance of all the interactions on the residential college campus to the education and maturation of students, I think of the students at Cumberland who have benefitted from daily direct contact with faculty and staff at the college—as well as from creating their own learning experiences and entertainment by working with other students.

I wish there was more documentation on the graduates of the College or University—beyond that on some of their best known graduates (such as Bert Combs, Kentucky governor from 1959-1963, and Edwin P. Morrow, governor from 1919-1923; Jean Ritchie, well-known ballad singer; Cratis Williams, often called the father of Appalachian studies; and a variety of military generals, an admiral, five college presidents, a Congressman and a host of ministers, missionaries, judges, medical doctors, teachers and attorneys). What I suspect I would find is long lists of people doing good work in the region and raising their children with respect for education and the importance of helping others. I would even find entrepreneurs who have made major changes in the region as school teachers, principals, and superintendents; as policemen and women, firefighters, lawyers, and judges; as medical doctors and nurses and dentists. What I am not likely to find are ones who have left the region and made fortunes establishing or operating large corporations—people like the alumnus of a small, elite, private college in central Kentucky who recently donated $250 million in stock to that college. What UC produces and has produced for over a hundred years are those who make up the backbone of a region that except for such people would be lost entirely to the ravages of poverty and deprivation.

It is hard to read *The Chronicle of Higher Education* or *Inside Higher Ed* (or either of my two other books) without recognizing that a lot of colleges are trying new approaches to surviving: mergers, selling to for-profits, developing a three-way partnership that involves corporations outside higher education carrying loans for the college, increasing course loads for faculty and staff, and reducing financial aid for students by recruiting only rich students. For some colleges, the only path to survival seems to be one of these extreme measures. Fortunately, however, there are colleges that are holding fast to their traditions at the same time they are exploring new options. I would not go so far as David Warren, President of National Association of Independent Colleges and Universities, who insists that "every private college plays a critical role and should be supported"—all the while he is warning, "The prospect of widespread school closings or mergers, though unlikely, is still a possibility if the market continues to be as dismal and credit lines are difficult to thaw."[3] But I do believe there is hope for most of those 1600 private colleges in the US still holding tightly to their dreams for the future. And I am pleased to offer UC as an example of how to make those dreams a reality.

During his inauguration speech in 1981, Taylor warned "A new day is dawning when many institutions will witness a downward drift in quality, balance, integrity and character." Since that speech, there have many days when various colleges, including Cumberland, have seen their futures threatened by economic downturns, declines in the numbers of traditional students, increased competition, and changes in federal and state rules and regulations that strain the capacity of small institutions to maintain compliance. Few have responded so well to such challenges as UC in maintaining "quality, balance, integrity and character."

What has Cumberland College done right? It has maintained a strong board of trustees who hired a capable president who is fully committed to the mission of the institution and knows how to raise money and recruit good faculty and staff and is married to someone who well represents the president when appropriate and can inspire him when he needs inspiration. One of the best explanations for the success of UC comes from the current president at College of the Ozarks in Missouri, and for many years previously president at Alice Lloyd College in Pippa Passes, Kentucky. Jerry Davis taught at Cumberland College, then attended graduate school at Ohio State and returned with his Ph.D in biology to teach at Cumberland from 1971 until 1976. Now that he has served in college presidencies for over 35 years, he is well qualified to analyze the success of Cumberland, and his analysis provides a good summary of its strengths: faculty are primarily full-time and strongly committed to the institution and its students; costs have been kept under control and a lot of financial aid keeps the College affordable for those who want to attend but do not have the money to afford such educational opportunities; the campus is one of the most attractive in the region; and new programs keep the options for the students broad and relevant. Davis agrees with others questioned: the greatest asset of UC is the stability of leadership, and its greatest threat in the future will be finding a new president who will maintain the vision and purpose of the institution as well as Taylor has.[4]

The board also considers the greatest threat to the University to be maintaining the kind of leadership that has led to its current state of stability. With possible changes in tax laws governing gift income and the unstable national economy, maintaining the institution that has been built is likely to grow increasingly difficult. What Cumberland has that other colleges don't is President Taylor, and the biggest threat to sustaining and growing the gift income is the possibility that, with all the traveling Taylor does, "the plane might go down." The board talks frequently about a succession plan and they know that Taylor has one—a plan that can be implemented if necessary but will be thoroughly tested (the expectation is) before then.[5] Davis and Oaks share the hope of many that the University will not just be able to maintain its current level of excellence but that, in Davis' words, "The College will be able to increase its endowment to assure the maintenance of the outstanding campus that has been built and the continuation of scholarships for the brightest students of limited means coming from the Appalachian region."

What is the University of the Cumberlands doing right? The institution continues to stay the course on which it was established and continues to find good people willing to sacrifice themselves to leading that cause. Len Schlesinger, President of Babson College, has said, "Colleges need to move away from the more and better approach and position themselves for the new economic reality by focusing on what they can do best."[6] UC continues to focus on what it can do best—bring education to a population of students who can most benefit from it even though they can least afford to pay for it. At the same time the University continues to move forward with new methods of providing that education, making what was good even better. The University was one of the first in the ACA to explore the use of the Internet to recruit new students; it is at the forefront of giving entering classes their own Facebook page to help unite and retain them; and online courses are becoming as prominent as the "in-seat" classes to promote learning. UC is not afraid to try the new while preserving the old.

I suspect that when Taylor does leave the presidency, he will be missed then more than he is appreciated now. In the meantime, President Taylor continues to offer all—other presidents and those in less prestigious positions—an example by which to live:

> **I've lived an exceptionally happy life, continually accompanied by good fortune with the exclusion of the knee buckling death of our son and my wife's health problems. I've, of course, possessed my share of painful memories, but I cling to optimism. There is true joy and a sense of fulfillment in being used for a purpose you recognize as a mighty one. How fleeting is fame; how temporary status? There is more to life than power, position and prestige. The secret to a happy life is investment in others. I want to be thoroughly used up when I die. As the athletes say, I want to leave it all on the floor. I want to make this candle burn as brightly as possible before handing it off to the next generation.[7]**

I remain among the many who hope his efforts to unite the best of the old and the best of the new will be well rewarded as he continues to build the University of the Cumberlands into the challenging future of higher education.

AUTHOR'S NOTES

In 1983, I became director of the Appalachian College Program (ACP), a program of the University of Kentucky which in 1990 became the Appalachian College Association (ACA). Taylor had been president of Cumberland College since 1980. Initially the program I ran focused on supporting faculty at 35 or so private colleges in central Appalachia, and I frequently visited the colleges to talk with faculty about the fellowships and other opportunities available through the program. In those early years, even though the faculty at Cumberland recognized the need for some campus beautification, they were frustrated by President Taylor's focus on the physical plant; they wanted him to focus on increasing their salaries and benefits and reducing their teaching loads—then at fifteen hours per semester (plus committee and advising responsibilities). Today they seem to have come to appreciate the physical plant of the campus, realizing that the attractiveness of a campus, like the first page of a book, is often the captivating attraction for potential students. Over the 25 years I led the ACA and the five years since, I have watched as the UC faculty increasingly have come to trust the president's judgment about financial expenditures and to appreciate the concern he expresses for the faculty and the changes he has implemented for their benefit.

When the ACP grew to include a focus on broad institutional goals (such as incorporating technology into instruction venues), the academic deans of the colleges formed a deans' council to help guide the growth of the organization. Early, who was then the dean for Academic Affairs at Cumberland College, became one of the most active of those deans. He was especially important to our work with technology and assessment since those were major concerns at Cumberland.

When the ACP left UK and became the ACA, a 501 (c) 3 organization, the presidents of the colleges formed the board, and President Taylor took an increasingly active role with the association, serving in a variety of offices, including chair, of that board. Some of the best advice I ever received about leading an organization came from the years he was the chair of my board. This information about the development of the association is important because it has been my experiences with multiple colleges and their presidents over 25 years that have given me some understanding of the problems such schools face and the leadership capacities of the presidents and others at those colleges. As I worked with the faculty of Cumberland College and watched as they and their administrators addressed various crises over the years, I gained insights into the operations of the College that continually increased my admiration of that institution. From 2008, when I retired from the ACA, to the current time, I have consulted with a variety of colleges and non-profit organizations, many outside the ACA network. Those experiences have strengthened my sense of appreciation for the work that Cumberland College has done and continues to do as the University of the Cumberlands.

In late 2011 and early 2012, I published two books: *Changing Course: Reinventing Colleges, Avoiding Closure* (Jossey-Bass) and *Cautionary Tales: Strategy Lessons from Struggling Colleges* (Stylus). The books were about colleges that closed (or were closed by actions of the accrediting agency, the church that had supported them, or the institution with which they had merged or to which they had been sold) and colleges that managed to bring themselves back from the edge of financial collapse by taking some major step (such as merging with another college/university, selling to a for-profit, cutting the number of employees and expanding the work loads of those remaining, or borrowing large amounts of money and building a physical plant that would attract wealthy students and allow the college to make financial aid almost non-existent).

Frequently, when I make presentations about that research, I am asked by representatives of colleges that have managed to make steady, though slow, progress over the years how their institutions can assure that such progress will continue to keep their schools financially sustainable. The obvious answer is they should keep doing what they are doing so long as it is working. The real question is what have they done that has resulted in steady progress. That is what a lot of the roughly 1600 private colleges across the country need to know.

Just within the network of the 37 colleges I served for 25 years as president of the ACA, there are several institutions that could be classified as thriving. Two have unique features that give them special standing in the world of small private colleges—and, therefore, make it virtually impossible to replicate their practices. The University of the South is one of about ten Episcopal colleges in the United States; its School of Theology is an official seminary for the denomination; and many of its alumni have distinguished themselves in professional fields and make significant financial contributions to the college. Berea College has maintained a loyal following of wealthy donors (many from large cities in the Northeast) since it was established in 1855 by focusing on recruiting only students from families with incomes at or near poverty level, most from Appalachia. Berea College has never charged tuition, guaranteeing each applicant accepted the equivalent of roughly $100,000 in educational benefits—an achievement made possible by its endowment of roughly a billion dollars. This book describes a college that has made steady progress over its 125-year history, but it has none of the special qualities often associated with thriving institutions: its endowment is less than $100 million; it has few rich alumni who might provide generous financial support; it has no special status among almost 50 colleges that are supported by its denominational affiliate; and it has held firm to its mission of service to the poor—even as it has broadened its curricula and procedures to include new populations (such as on-campus adult learners and online students of all ages).

With the publication of my two earlier books, I had a framework in which to evaluate an institution: I look at its leadership, its funding base, and its culture. When I approached President Taylor in late 2012 to ask for his support in this new venture, he agreed to provide whatever information about the institution he could, and he opened his files containing copies of his communications with trustees and speeches he has given. He did warn me, after showing me a wall of bookcases containing several thousand books on higher education that he has read over the years, that some of his letters and speeches might contain undocumented phrases from some of those books that he remembered at the time; he advised me to research any that might sound as though they came from a source other than him.

When I did that research, I was pleased to find that there were none that were quotes from a source not referenced.

Taylor and I talked about the fact that the University was in the process of producing a book on its history while the book I was proposing would be one focused on the less tangible aspects of the institution—the philosophies and feelings people have about the institution, not the historical development of it. My discussions with various faculty, students, staff, alumni, etc. would not be considered formal interviews but conversations focusing on the strengths and weaknesses of the University. Data reported would be important as a way of confirming what faculty and administrators and students believe true.

Finally, it is important to note that Taylor stressed the study I was proposing would clearly have to be mine and that, while he might look at some early drafts of a manuscript, the final version would be mine alone, that he would claim "no pride of ownership"—thereby encouraging me at the same time he cautioned me: any errors or omissions, any compliments or criticisms would be due to my research and selection of information to share; he would not try to steer me toward one set of data or another or toward one story or another. Humility keeps the University from boasting about its own accomplishments; it is an honor to be able to declare the value of this small, private institution that good people have built for good reasons. I believe there is much that many institutions can learn from this one little-known university on a hill.

ACKNOWLEDGEMENTS

I have had many mentors throughout my career in higher education, but none was more generous in providing me with advice and assistance than William G. Bowen. Bowen was president of the Andrew W. Mellon Foundation during most of the years I was president of the ACA, and during that time he was one of the strongest advocates for the small private colleges in the mountains of Appalachia. He understands their struggles and their value. Despite warnings from others about the dangers of associating with "drowning colleges," Bowen encouraged me to pursue my interest in analyzing why colleges fail and how they can close with grace, even writing the Foreword for one of my books. And there were others with strong credentials in the world of higher education who encouraged my work by contributing essays for the books, including Robert Zemsky, Mike Puglishi, Elizabeth Hayford, Richard Johnson, Mary Linda Armacost, Richard Kneipper, Barbara Hatton and Arthur Levine. Without their contributed chapters, I suspect those first two books would never have been published. Without the continuing friendship of such people and our frequent discussions about the state of higher education, I might have lost interest in the struggles of the small colleges.

When considering whether to prepare a third book, I decided that perhaps a better way to help small private colleges facing increasingly hostile forces was to focus, not on those that closed or almost closed, but on those that have faced major obstacles over many years but have maintained financial stability, even growing stronger during the past few decades when the national economy and public opinions have provided little or no encouragement. And when I decided to focus my attention first on a college I had watched for at least three decades, almost everyone on that campus assisted in the preparation of the book. In listing names here, I am sure I have failed to include some; and, in many cases, I did not even take the name of the student or staff person I questioned as I was crossing the campus. What I found most interesting is that everyone I spoke with responded to my questions graciously. I never had the response that I often had in preparing my other books: "I can't talk to you about this college." Even trustees at other schools would often say, "What I know about this college is confidential." At UC, everyone I spoke with had the same message: "The University of the Cumberlands is a caring campus and we are proud to talk about it."

President Taylor gave me access to the documents I requested and permission to interview anyone on or off the campus who I thought might have opinions worthy of considering. He gave me his cell phone number and invited me to call him at any time.

Taylor's chief assistant and Vice President for Institutional Advancement, Sue Wake, is one of the most amazing people I have ever met. She is always available—no matter what time of the week or day I call; always congenial—no matter how busy her schedule might be; always informed—no matter what question I ask; always willing to do more—no matter what I expect; and always empathetic—no matter how bad or how good the news. On every visit I made to the campus, Wake and the two who assist her, Alice Bowling and Sherry Roaden, welcomed me and assisted with scheduling visits to the other offices, loaned me their computers, helped me copy materials from the files, and loaded my car with books the president thought I should read to understand his philosophy of leadership.

Between mid-December, 2012, and January 3, 2013, I met with President Taylor and his vice-president/assistant; Todd Yetter, Chair of the Biology Department; Tom Frazier, Chair of English; Larry Cockrum, Vice President of Academic Affairs, who is responsible for academic programs on the campus, at the extension centers, and online; Michael Colegrove, Vice President of Student Services, who ensures that students have support in areas of housing, recreation and leadership; Lisa Bartram, Director of Student Activities; Kay Manning, the office manager for development programs; Susan Weaver, Director of Teaching and Learning, and Donnie Grimes, Vice President of Information Technology. Later that month, I received statistical information from Chuck Dupier, III, the registrar for the University and the person responsible for institutional research. Erica Harris in the office of admissions provided data on freshmen students.

Between February and March, I received information from a variety of administrators on the campus, including Jana Bailey, Vice President of Finance, who oversees the financial management of the University's investments and banking; Kyle Gilbert, Vice President of Operations, who oversees not only the general operations but also the physical plant and lands, including planning for future development; Steve Morris, Vice President of Business, including human resources and business operations; Steve Allen, Vice President for Financial Planning, including financial aid and support. Brad Hall, another assistant to the president, read early drafts of the book, corrected my factual errors and provided relevant data and comments. Later in March, I spoke with Dinah Taylor, wife of the president, and former vice-presidents Joe Early and Don Good—all of whom told interesting stories about their lives as part of the College.

In early April, I met with Randy Vernon, Director of the athletic program; Tom Fish, Associate Dean of Academic Affairs; Sara Ash, biology professor; Julie Tan, Chair of the Chemistry Department; Peggy Woods, Dean of Student Employees, and her assistant Mirissa Crumpston; Pearl Baker, Director of Human Resources; Janice Wren, Director of the library; and Rick Fleenor, Director of Church Relations and International Relations. In late April, I spoke with Jim Oaks, the chair of the board, and on May 1, Debbie Harp explained to me how, as a one-person office, she provides career services to the students.

While not all of these representatives of UC are quoted or referenced directly in the book, all provided valuable information, many reinforcing what I had already learned from others.

During my work on the book, I spoke with a variety of leaders in the world of higher education who have long known the work of Cumberland College and its work as UC. Those who offered information used in this book were Belle Wheelan, President of the Southern Association of Colleges and Schools (SACS); Joe Stepp, President of Alice Lloyd College; Jerry C. Davis, President of the College of the Ozarks; Bruce Heilman,

Alice W. Brown

President Emeritus of the University of Richmond; and George Dehne of George Dehne and Associates.

To all of these people and many not noted here, I am deeply appreciative of the opportunity to work with you to tell the story of Cumberland Colleges (now University of the Cumberlands).

ENDNOTES

Preface

[1] Charles Huckabee, "Saint Paul's College, in Virginia, Reportedly Will Close," *Chronicle of Higher Education* (June 3, 2013). http://chronicle.com/blogs/ticker/ st-pauls-college-uin-virginia-reported-will-close/61261 (accessed July 23, 2013); Nick Desantis, "Virginia Orders Unaccredited U. of Northern Virginia to Shut Down," *Chronicle of Higher Education* (July 22, 2013). http://chronicle.com/blogs/ ticker/virginia-orders-unaccredited-u-of-northern-virginia-to-shut-down/63441 (accessed July 23, 2013); Desantis, "Chancellor U., a For-Profit College in Ohio, Will Close Its Doors," *Chronicle of Higher Education* (July 8, 2013). http:// chronicle.com/blogs/ticker/chancellor-u-a-for-profit-college-in-ohio-will-close-its- doors/62743 (accessed July 23, 2013).

[2] Ray Brown, "List of Colleges that Have Closed, Merged, or Changed their Names." http://www2.westminster-mo.edu/wc_users/ . . . /staff/ . . . /closedcollegeindex. htm (accessed July 23, 2013).

[3] Goldie Blumenstyk, "Declines in Tuition Revenue Leave Many Colleges Financial- ly Squeezed," *Chronicle of Higher Education* (January 10, 2013). http://chronicle. com/blogs/bottomline/declines-in-tuition-revenue-leave-many-colleges-financial- ly-squeezed (accessed February 13, 2013).

[4] Williamsburg Institute, "Articles of Incorporation," April 8, 1888, in James H. Tay- lor and Elizabeth Sue Wake, eds., *A Bright Shining City Set on a Hill: a Centennial History* (Williamsburg, KY: Cumberland College, 1988), 22.

[5] George Keller, *Transforming a College: The Story of a Little-Known College's Strategic Climb to National Distinction* (Baltimore, MD: Johns Hopkins University Press,

2004), 10.

[6] James Taylor, letter to author. February 11, 2013.

[7] Clayton M. Christensen, Clayton M. and Henry J. Eyring, *The Innovative University: Changing the DNA of Higher Education from the Inside Out* (San Francisco, CA: Jossey-Bass, 2011), 18.

[8] Oliver Wendell Holmes, Jr., letter to Elmer Gertz (March 1, 1899). Quoted in Keller, 2004.

Chapter I: Region

[1] CBS News, "Reporters Risks Lives to Expose Corruption." May 3, 2012, http://www.cbsnews.com/2102-18560_162-57427302.html (accessed July 23, 2013).

[2] *Corbin Times-Tribune*, "14 Arrested in Drug Roundup" and "1,000 Reward Offered for Robbery Info," April 2, 2013; *Corbin News Journal*, "A Dozen Dealers Targeted in Latest Whitley Drug Raid," May 3, 2012.

[3] Census Viewer 2010, "Population of Whitley County, KY and Williamsburg, KY Population," http:censusviewer.com/county/KY/Whitley (accessed May 18, 2013).

[4] Kentucky State Government. Population of Whitley County, Kentucky, Census 2010 and 2000 Interactive Map, Demographics, Statistics, Graphs, Quick Facts. Whitley County, 2012, http:/Kentuckyp20.KY.gov/reports/CPG_2012_Whitley.pdf (accessed May 18, 2013).

[5] Southern Education Foundation (SEF), *The Worst of Times: Extreme Poverty in the United States, 2009 (Atlanta, GA: SEF, 2010)*, 3-8, 20.

[6] Thomas Miller, "Speak Your Piece: Proximity Matters," *Daily Yonder*, November 2012, http://www.dailyyonder.com/speak-your-piece-proximity-matters/2012/11/07/4914 (accessed November 13, 2012).

[7] Ibid.

[8] Brad Hall, correspondence to author, February 22, 2013.

[9] SEF, 9.

[10] *Corbin News Journal*, "University of the Cumberlands Contributes to Williamsburg and Whitley County," December 5, 2012.

[11] Ibid.

Chapter 2: Leadership

[1] Belle Wheelan, correspondence to author, January 10, 2013.

[2] Hall.

[3] Jim Oaks, telephone conversation with author, April 15, 2013.

[4] Bruce Heilman, telephone conversation with author, March 14, 2013.

[5] James Taylor, Presentation to Southern Association Reaffirmation Committee, Williamsburg, KY, April 2, 1995.

[6] J. Taylor, correspondence to author, January 2, 2013.

[7] J. Taylor, "A College President's Perspective of Fund Raising, or A Peek at the President," Speech for National Society of Fund Raising Executives, Lexington, KY, May 20, 1987.

[8] J. Taylor, correspondence to author, March 20, 2013.

[9] J. Taylor, Speech for Council of Independent Colleges Meeting, January 6, 2007.

[10] Hall.

[11] J. Taylor, Presentation to Southern Association.

[12] Don Good, telephone conversation with author, March 19, 2013.

[13] Oaks.

[14] William G. Bowen, *Lessons Learned: Reflections of a University President* (Princeton, NJ: Princeton University Press, 2011).

[15] Henry N. Drewry and Humphrey Doermann, *Stand and Prosper: Private Black Colleges and Their Students* (Princeton, NJ: Princeton University Press, 2001).

[16] J. Taylor, "A College President's Perspective."

[17] Heilman.

[18] Keller.

[19] James H. Taylor and Elizabeth Sue Wake, eds., *A Bright Shining City Set on a Hill: a Centennial History* (Williamsburg, KY: Cumberland College, 1988), 22.

[20] Joe Stepp, telephone conversation with author, January 16, 2013.

[21] Joseph Early, correspondence to author, March 1, 2013.

[22] Dinah Taylor, telephone conversation with author, March 30, 2013.

[23] J. Taylor, "A New Day Dawning," Inauguration Speech, May 2, 1981.

[24] J.Taylor, correspondence to author, March 25, 2013.

[25] A Neilson Waldemire, *The Endangered Sector* (NY: Columbia University Press, 1979) in James Taylor, "Private Higher Education in the 1980s," Speech, March 11, 1981.

[26] Hugh Hawkins, "The Making of the Liberal Arts College Identity," Daedalus, 128.1. 1999. Quoted in Francis Oakley, "The Liberal Arts College: Identity, Variety, and Destiny," in American Council of Learned Societies, *Liberal Arts College in American Higher Education: Challenges and Opportunities*. Occasional Paper #59, 2005: 15-21.

[27] Tajuana Cheshier, "Lamburth's Fall: Many Decisions Over Many Years Led to Uni-

versity's Closure", Jackson, TN, *Jackson Sun*. June 26, 2001, http://pqasb.pqarchiv-er.com/jacksonsun/access/2388068981.html?FMT=FT&FMTS=ABS:FT&type=current&fmac=2c0c499b4fcf9c3f0fe7c6fb52851ead&date=Jun+26%2C+2011&author=Tajuana+Cheshier&desc=Lambuth%27s+fall%3A+Many+decisions+over+many+years+led+to+university%27s+closure (accessed January 18, 2013).

[28] J. Taylor, "Private Education in the 1980s."

[29] J. Taylor, "Faith Isn't for the Faint Hearted," Speech, Southern Baptist Colleges and Universities, 1988.

[30] Hall.

[31] J. Taylor, correspondence, January 2, 2013.

[32] Clark Kerr, *The Uses of the University*, 5th ed., Cambridge, MA: Harvard University Press, 2001, 29-30.

[33] J. Taylor, on-campus conversation with author, December 18, 2012.

[34] "20 Years of Visionary Leadership," Paper Celebrating Special Event, 2001.

[35] D. Taylor.

[36] Alice W. Brown and Sandra Ballard, *Changing Course: Reinventing Colleges, Avoiding Closure: New Directions for Higher Education*, Number 156, Winter (San Franscisco, CA: Jossey-Bass, 2011).

[37] D. Taylor.

[38] Marvin Lazerson. "The Disappointment of Success: Higher Education after World War II," in *The History of Higher Education*, 3rd ed., eds. Harold S. Wechsler, Lester F. Goodchild, and Linda Eisenmann, Boston, MA: Pearson Custom Publishing, 2007.

[39] Lewis B. Mayhew. *Surviving the Eighties: Strategies and Procedures for Solving Fiscal and Enrollment Problems*. San Francisco, CA: Jossey-Bass, 1980, quoted in John R. Thelin, *A History of American Higher Education* (Baltimore, MD: Johns Hopkins

University Press, 2004), 319.

[40] University of the Cumberlands, "Dr. Joe Early Retires," *Cumberland Today*, Summer, 2002, 2 & 7.

[41] Peter F. Drucker, *The Essential Drucker: The Best of Sixty Years of Peter Drucker's Essential Writings on Management* (New York, NY: Harper Collins, 2001).

[42] John P. Kotter, *What Leaders Really Do*, Cambridge, MA: Harvard Business Review, 1999, http://www.Kotterinternational.comn/our-principles/change-leadership (accessed February 28, 2013).

[43] J. Early.

[44] Stepp.

[45] University of the Cumberlands, "Early Retires," 2.

[46] J. Taylor, correspondence, March 20, 2013.

[47] University of the Cumberlands, "Early Retires," 7.

[48] Good.

[49] Rob Jenkins, "What Makes a Good Leader?" *Chronicle of Higher Education*, February 19, 2013, http://chronicle.com/blogs/onhiring/what-makes-a-good-leader/36725 (accessed February 19, 2013).

[50] J. Early.

[51] J. Taylor, conversation, 2012.

[52] Alice W. Brown, *Cautionary Tales: Strategy Lessons from Struggling Colleges* (Sterling, VA: Stylus Publishing, 2012).

[53] Bowen, 83.

[54] Hall.

[55] James L. Fisher, *The Board and the President*, New York, NY: Macmillan Publishing, 1991.

[56] J. Taylor, Letter to Trustees, March 31, 2010.

[57] J. Taylor, "A College President's Perspective."

[58] J. Taylor, conversation, 2012.

[59] J. Taylor, 2007.

Chapter 3: Funding

[1] J. Taylor, "A College President's Perspective."

[2] Pearson Education, Inc., "What Presidents Think: A 2013 Survey of Four-Year College Presidents," *Chronicle of Higher Education*, March 13, 2013, http://www.chronicle.com/WhatPresidentsThink_Pearson2013.pdf (accessed May 1, 2013).

[3] J. Taylor, "Tuition, Finance, and Fund Raising: Issues for Private Institutions," Speech at SACS Meeting, Dallas, TX, December 7, 1992.

[4] J. Taylor, "Development Techniques in a Recessionary Economy," *The Southern Baptist Educator*, March 8, 1992.

[5] Taylor and Wake.

[6] James H. Taylor, A Proposal Respectfully Submitted to Dr. J.M. Boswell and the Cumberland College Board of Trustees, n.d.

[7] J. Taylor, Letter to Trustees, February 1, 2010.

[8] Kay Manning, on-campus conversation with author, January 3, 2013.

[9] J. Taylor, "The Donor Matrix: Recency, Frequency, Amount, Psychographics & Demographics," Lecture, Vanderbilt University, April 22, 2000.

[10] J. Taylor, "Development Techniques."

[11] Shannon Warmoth, *Putting Something Back*, August-December, 2001.

[12] J. Early.

[13] J. Taylor, correspondence to author, February 11, 2013.

[14] Cumberland College, *Promises to Keep: Cumberland College*, 1983.

[15] University of the Cumberlands, In Pursuit of *Vita Abundantior*: The Strategic Plan of the University of the Cumberlands, 2004.

[16] University of the Cumberlands, Strategic Plan 2020, 2011.

[17] Fr. Theodore Hesburg, in Peggy Mathaba Neube, "A Rhetorial Analysis of Theodore Hesburgh's Fund-Raising Speeches for the University of Notra Dame," Ph.D. diss, Andrews University, June 2002, 3-4, http://www.andrews.edu/~freed/resources_qdtations.html (accessed July 27, 2013).

[18] J. Taylor, conversation, 2012.

[19] Ibid.

[20] J. Taylor, Presentation for Board, April 20-21, 1995.

[21] Lawrence Cockrum, on-campus conversation with author, January 3, 2013.

[22] Edward J. Kormondy, and Kent M. Keith, *Nine University Presidents Who Saved Their Institutions: The Difference in Effective Administration*, Lewiston, NY: The Edwin Mellen Press, 2008.

[23] J. Taylor, Letter to Trustees, October 31, 2010.

[24] J. Taylor, Letter, March 31, 2010.

[25] J. Taylor, SACS.

[26] J. Early.

[27] Ibid.

Chapter 4: Culture

[1] Williamsburg Institute, "Articles of Incorporation," 17.

[2] Taylor and Wake, 353.

[3] Christensen and Eyring, 162.

[4] MSNBC, "Dozens Rally for Student Expelled for Being Gay," http://www.msnbc.msn.com/id/31066137/media-kit/http://g.msn.com/AIPRIV/en-us (accessed December 10, 2012).

[5] Lisabeth Hughes Abramson, Opinion of the Supreme Court of Kentucky, 2008-SC-000253-TG, April 22, 2010, 2.

[6] Adam Sulfridge, "UC Officials Mum about Turning Choir Away," Corbin *Times-Tribune*, July 9, 2009, http://thetimestribune.com/local/x1048573922/UC-officials-mum-about-turning-choir-away (accessed Dec. 15, 2012).

[7] Derek Bok, *Our Underachieving Colleges: A Candid Look at How Much Students Learn and Why They Should Be Learning More* (Princeton, NJ: Princeton University Press, 2006), quoted in Christensen and Eyring, 355.

[8] Hart Research Associates, "Survey of Part-Time and Adjunct Higher Education Faculty," in American Federation of Teachers. *American Academic*, Vol. 2, March 2010, 3-15, http://www.aft.org/pdfs/highered/aa_partimefaculty0310.pdf (accessed February 18, 2013).

[9] Tom Fish, on-campus conversation with author, April 1, 2013.

[10] J. Early.

[11] Todd Yetter, on-campus conversation with author, January 2, 2013.

[12] J. Taylor, "A College President's Perspective."

[13] Fisher, 281.

[14] James L. Fisher and James V. Koch, *Presidential Leadership: Making a Difference.* In American Council on Education Oryx Press Series on Higher Education (Phoenix, Arizona: The Oryx Press, 1996), 28.

[15] Susan Resneck Pierce, *On Being Presidential: A Guide for College and University Leaders* (SanFrancisco, CA: Jossey Bass Press, 2012), 113-114, 137.

[16] Keven Kiley, "Moody's Report Calls into Question All Traditional University Revenue Sources," *Inside Higher Ed,* January 17, 2013, http://www.insidehighered.com/print/news/2013/01/17/moodys-report-calls-question-all-traditional-university-revenue-sources (accessed February 13, 2013).

[17] J. Taylor, "A College President's Perspective."

[18] Julie Tan, on-campus conversation with author, April 2, 2013.

[19] Edward J. Kormondy and Kent M. Keith. *Nine University Presidents Who Saved Their Institutions: The Difference in Effective Administration* (Lewiston, NY: The Edwin Mellen Press, 2008), 85.

[20] J. Taylor, correspondence to author, February 7, 2013.

[21] J. Early.

[22] Sue Wake, on-campus conversation with author, April 2, 2013.

[23] Fisher and Koch, 154.

[24] J. Taylor, "Donor Matrix."

[25] J. Taylor, "A College President's Perspective."

[26] Warmouth, 7.

[27] Sara Ash, on-campus conversation with author, April 1, 2013.

[28] Appalachian College Association, Data on Member Colleges from the US Department of Education, National Center for Educational Statistics, Integrated Postsecondary Education Data System (IPEDS) for 2010-2011.

[29] J. Taylor, "Speech to Faculty and Administrative Staff," n.d.

[30] Quoted in Kerr, 24.

[31] Keller, 1.

[32] Christensen and Eyring, 353.

[33] Cockrum.

[34] Susan Weaver, correspondence to author, March 21, 2013.

[35] Pat Summers and Sally Jenkins, *Sum It Up: 1,098 Victories, a Couple of Irrelevant Losses, and a Life in Perspective* (New York, NY: Crown Publishing Group, 2013), Kindle edition.

[36] Corbin *News Journal*, "UC Contributes."

[37] Weaver, March 21.

[38] Taylor, letter, March 31.

[39] Taylor, correspondence, March 25.

[40] Ibid.

[41] Christensen and Eyring, xxiii.

[42] Shankar Vedantam, "Elite Colleges Struggle to Recruit Smart, Low-Income Kids," Morning Edition. January 9. http://www.wlrn.org/people/shankar-vedantam (accessed January 9, 2013).

[43] Ibid.

[44] Steve Allen, Data on Pell Grant Recipients, http://www2.ed.gov/programs/fpg/index/html (accessed February 22, 2013).

[45] Erica Harris, Data on Freshmen Demographics, February 22, 2013.

[46] Linda Scott DeRosier, *A Woman's Journey: Creeker* (Lexington, KY: The University Press of Kentucky, 1999), 122-124.

[47] Ernest T. Pascarella and Patrick T. Terenzini. "Alumni Study for the Appalachian College Association," 2001.

[48] University of the Cumberlands, "Our Freshmen Are Good But Our Juniors Are Even Better, *Cumberland Alumni Magazine* (Winter 2010), 6.

[49] Michael Colegrove, on-campus conversation with the author, January 2, 2013.

[50] Ibid.

[51] Fish.

[52] Arthur Levine and Diane Dean, "Today's Students: Same as Always, but More So," *Chronicle of Higher Education,* September 10, 2012, http:chronicle.com/article/Todays-Students-Same-as/134234 (accessed February 19, 2013).

[53] Rick Fleenor, on-campus conversation with author, March 5, 2013.

[54] Ibid.

[55] Taylor and Wake, 54-55.

[56] Bok, 172.

[57] University of the Cumberlands, Office of Assessment 2011-2012 Graduate Student Form MAEd, MAT, EdS Code 952 Summary, n.d.

[58] Kristin Gotch, "UC Vice President of Academic Affairs Speaks for the Value of

a Well-Rounded Education," Media Release, September 10, 2012, http://www.ucumberlands.edu/media/release.php?rk=1410 (accessed February 20, 2013).

[59] Christensen and Eyring, 385.

[60] Gary Bonvillian and Robert Murphy, *The Liberal Arts College Adapting to Change: The Survival of Small Schools* (NewYork, NY: Garland Publishing, Inc. 1996).

[61] Marvin Lazerson, "The Disappointment of Success: Higher Education after World War II," in *The History of Higher Education*, 3rd ed., eds. Harold S. Wechsler, Lester F. Goodchild, and Linda Eisenmann, 792-800 (Boston, MA: Pearson Custom Publishing, 2007).

[62] Peggy Woods, on-campus conversation with author, April 2, 2013.

[63] Cockrum.

[64] Chuck Dupier III, correspondence to author, January 11, 2013.

[65] Weaver, correspondence, March 21, 2013.

[66] Susan Weaver, correspondence to author, April 2, 2013.

[67] Appalachian College Association.

[68] George D. Kuh, "Built to Engage: Liberal Arts Colleges and Effective Educational Practice," in American Council of Learned Societies, *Liberal Arts Colleges in American Higher Education: Challenges and Opportunities* (Occasional Paper #59, 2005), 146.

[69] University of the Cumberlands, Annual Assessment Report 2011-2012: Career Services (September 5. 2012).

[70] Taylor, letter, March 31, 2013.

[71] Randy Vernon, on-campus conversation with author, April 2, 2013.

[72] Woods.

[73] University of the Cumberlands, "Whitley Native Becomes First Dean of Student Employment at University of the Cumberlands," Media Release, May 7, 2010.

[74] Woods.

[75] Wake.

[76] Stepp.

[77] University of the Cumberlands, "Annual Assessment Report 2011-2012: Leadership and Community Service," September 5, 2012.

[78] *Corbin News Journal*, "UC Contributes."

[79] Ibid.

[80] Taylor and Wake, 23.

[81] J. Taylor, correspondence, March 25, 2013.

[82] J. Early.

[83] Kyle Gilbert, Information on Buildings and Grounds, February 22, 2013.

[84] J. Taylor, Faculty/Staff Speech, August 21, 2009.

[85] George Dehne, telephone conversation with author, January 21, 2013.

[86] Taylor and Wake.

[87] Blain W. Early III, Letter to Robert C. Berness, University Counsel, Princeton University, November 19, 2009.

[88] Bishop of Seville quoted in Jerold Panas, *Board Room Verities: A Celebration of Trusteeship with Some Guides and Techniques to Govern By*, 2012.

[89] J. Taylor, letter, January 2.

Chapter 5: Future Goals

[1] Taylor, Presentation to Southern Association.

[2] University of the Cumberlands, "Strategic Plan 2020."

[3] James Martin and James E. Samels & Associates. *Turnaround: Leading Stressed Colleges and Universities to Excellence* (Baltimore, MD: Johns Hopkins University Press, 2009); Hall.

[4] Ibid.

[5] Pearson Education, Inc.

[6] David Breneman, "What Colleges Can Learn from Recessions Past," *Chronicle of Higher Education*, October 10, 2008, http://chronicle.com/article/What-Colleges-Can-Learn-Fro/16846 (accessed June 9, 2013).

[7] University of the Cumberlands, "Strategic Plan 2020."

[8] J. Taylor, Speech for CIC Meeting.

[9] J. Taylor, letter, March 20, 2013.

Conclusions

[1] 204 Alexander Astin and Calvin Lee, *The Invisible Colleges: A Profile of Small, Private Colleges with Limited Resources* (New York, NY: McGraw-Hill Publishing, 1974), 65.

[2] Richard Hersh and John Merrow, *Declining by Degrees: Higher Education at Risk* (New York, NY: Palgrave Macmillan, 2005), 24.

[3] Kathleen Kingsbury and Laura Fitzpatrick, "Colleges Learn to Navigate the Credit Crunch," *Time* (December 11, 2008), http://www.time.com/time/magazine/article/0,9171,1865949,00.html (accessed January 18, 2013).

[4] Jerry Davis, correspondence to author, March 4-8, 2013.

[5] Oaks.

[6] Quoted in Christensen and Eyring, 353.

[7] J. Taylor, letter, January 2, 2013.

BIBLIOGRAPHY

Abramson, Lisabeth Hughes. Opinion of the Supreme Court of Kentucky, 2008—SC-000253-TG. April 22, 2010.

Allen, Steve. Data on Pell Grant Recipients from http://www2.ed.gov/programs/fpg/index/html. February 22, 2013.

Appalachian College Association. Data on Member Colleges from the US Department of Education. National Center for Educational Statistics. Integrated Postsecondary Education Data System (IPEDS) for 2010-2011. June, 2012.

Astin, Alexander and Calvin Lee. *The Invisible Colleges: A Profile of Small, Private Colleges with Limited Resources.* New York, NY: McGraw-Hill Publishing, 1974.

Blumenstyk, Goldie. "Declines in Tuition Revenue Leave Many Colleges Financially Squeezed." *Chronicle of Higher Education,* January 10, 2013. http://chronicle.com/blogs/bottomline/declines-in-tuition-revenue-leave-many-colleges-financially-squeezed (accessed February 13, 2013).

Bonvillian, Gary and Robert Murphy. *The Liberal Arts College Adapting to Change: The Survival of Small Schools.* New York, NY: Garland Publishing, Inc., 1996.

Bowen, William G. *Lessons Learned: Reflections of a University President.* Princeton, NJ: Princeton University Press, 2011.

Breneman, David. "What Colleges Can Learn from Recessions Past."

Chronicle of Higher Education, October 10, 2008. http://chronicle.com/article/What-Colleges-Can-Learn-Fro/16846 (accessed June 9, 2013).

Brown, Alice W. and Sandra Ballard. *Changing Course: Reinventing Colleges, Avoiding Closure: New Directions for Higher Education,* Number 156 (Winter). San Franscisco, CA: Jossey-Bass, 2011.

Brown, Alice W. *Cautionary Tales: Strategy Lessons from Struggling Colleges.* Sterling, VA: Stylus Publishing, 2012.

Brown, Ray. "List of Colleges that Have Closed, Merged, or Changed their Names." http://www2.westminster-mo.edu/wc_users/ . . . /staff/ . . . /closedcollegeindex.htm (accessed July 23, 2013).

CBS News. "Reporters Risks Lives to Expose Corruption." May 3, 2012. http://www.cbsnews.com/2102-18560_162-57427302.html (accessed July 23, 2013).

Census Viewer. Population of Whitley County, KY and Williamsburg, KY Population. 2010. http:censusviewer.com/county/KY/Whitley (accessed May 18, 2013).

Cheshier, Tajuana. "Lamburth's Fall: Many Decisions Over Many Years Led to University's Closure." Jackson, TN, *Jackson Sun,* June 26, 2001. http://pqasb.pqarchiver.com/jacksonsun/access/2388068981.html?FMT=FT&FMTS=ABS:FT&type=current&fmac=2c0c499b4fcf9c3f0fe7c6fb52851ead&date=Jun+26%2C+2011&author=Tajuana+Cheshier&desc=Lambuth%27s+fall%3A+Many+decisions+over+many+years+led+to+university%27s+closure (accessed January 18, 2013).

Christensen, Clayton M. and Henry J. Eyring. *The Innovative University: Changing the DNA of Higher Education from the Inside Out.* San Francisco, CA: Jossey-Bass, 2011.

Corbin News Journal. "University of the Cumberlands Contributes to Williamsburg and Whitley County." December 5, 2012.

Cumberland College. "Promises to Keep: Cumberland College. Long-Range Plan," 1983.

_____. "Cumberland College Mountain Outreach Program: How It All Began." Pamphlet. N.d.

DeRosier, Linda Scott. *A Woman's Journey: Creeker.* Lexington, KY: The University Press of Kentucky, *1999.*

Desantis, Nick. "Virginia Orders Unaccredited U. of Northern Virginia to Shut Down." *Chronicle of Higher Education,* July 22, 2013. http://chronicle.com/blogs/ticker/virginia-orders-unaccredited-u-of-northern-virginia-to-shut-down/63441 (accessed July 23, 2013).

_____. "Chancellor U., a For-Profit College in Ohio, Will Close Its Doors." *Chronicle of Higher Education,* July 8, 2013. http://chronicle.com/blogs/ticker/chancellor-u-a-for-profit-college-in-ohio-will-close-its-doors/62743 (accessed July 23, 2013).

Drewry, Henry N., and Humphrey Doermann. 2001. *Stand and Prosper: Private Black Colleges and Their Students.* Princton, NJ: Princeton University Press, 2001.

Drucker, Peter F. *The Essential Drucker: The Best of Sixty Years of Peter Drucker's Essential Writings on Management.* New York, NY: Harper Collins, 2001.

Early, W. Blain, III. 2009. Letter to Robert C. Berness, University Counsel, Princeton University, November 19, 2009.

Fain, Paul. "ACE Commissioned Report on Disruption and Adult Students." *Inside Higher Ed,* January 21, 2013. http://www.insidehighered.com/news/2013/01/21/ace-commissioned-report-disruption-and-adult-students (accessed January 21, 2013).

Fisher, James L. *The Board and the President.* New York, NY: Macmillan Publishing, 1991.

Fisher, James L. and James V. Koch. *Presidential Leadership: Making a Difference.* In American Council on Education Oryx Press Series on Higher Education. Phoenix, AZ: The Oryx Press, 1996.

Friedman, Thomas L. "The Professors' Big Stage." *New York Times,* March 5, 2013. http://www.nytimes.com/2013/03/06/opinion/friedman-the-professors-big-stage.html?src=me&ref=general&_r=0 (accessed March 11, 2013).

Gotch, Kristin. "UC Vice President of Academic Affairs Speaks for the Value of a Well-Rounded Education." Media release, September 10, 2012. http://www.ucumberlands.edu/media/release.php?rk=1410 (accessed February 20, 2013).

Hart Research Associates. "Survey of Part-Time and Adjunct Higher Education Faculty. January." In American Federation of Teachers. *American Academic,* Vol. 2, March 2010: 3-15. http://www.aft.org/pdfs/highered/aa_partimefaculty0310.pdf (accessed February 18, 2013).

Hawkins, Hugh. "The Making of the Liberal Arts College Identity." Daedalus, 128.1. 1999. Quoted in Francis Oakley, "The Liberal Arts College: Identity, Variety, and Destiny," in American Council of Learned Societies, *Liberal Arts College in American Higher Education: Challenges and Opportunities.* Occasional Paper #59, 2005: 15-21.

Hesburg, Theodore. Quoted in Peggy Mathaba Neube, "A Rhetorial Analysis of Theodore Hesburgh's Fund-Raising Speeches for the University of Notre Dame." Ph.D. diss, Andrews University, June, 2002. http://www.andrews.edu/~freed/resources_qdtations.html (accessed July 27, 2013).

Hersh, Richard and John Merrow. *Declining by Degrees: Higher Education at Risk.* New York, NY: Palgrave Macmillan, 2005.

Holmes, Oliver Wendell, Jr. Letter to Elmer Gertz, March 1.1899. Quoted in Keller, 2004.

Huckabee, Charles. "Saint Paul's College, in Virginia, Reportedly Will Close." *Chronicle of Higher Education,* June 3, 2013. http://chronicle. com/blogs/ticker/st-pauls-college-uin-virginia-reported-will-close/61261 (accessed July 23, 2013).

Jenkins, Rob. "What Makes a Good Leader?" *Chronicle of Higher Education,* February 19, 2013. http://chronicle.com/blogs/onhiring/what-makes-a-good-leader/36725? (accessed February 24, 2013).

Keller, George. *Transforming a College: The Story of a Little-Known College's Strategic Climb to National Distinction.* Baltimore, MD: Johns Hopkins University Press, 2004.

Kentucky State Government. Population of Whitley County, Kentucky. Census 2010 and 2000 Interactive Map, Demographics, Statistics, Graphs, Quick Facts. Whitley County, 2012. http:/Kentuckyp20. KY.gov/reports/CPG_2012_Whitley.pdf (accessed May 18, 2013).

Kerr, Clark. *The Uses of the University*. 5th ed. Cambridge, MA: Harvard University Press, 2001.

Kiley, Kevin. "Moody's Report Calls into Question All Traditional University Revenue Sources." *Inside Higher Ed,* January 17, 2013. http://www.insidehighered.com/print/news/2013/01/17/moodys-report-calls-question-all-traditional-university-revenue-sources (accessed February 13, 2013).

Kingsbury, Kathleen and Laura Fitzpatrick. "Colleges Learn to Navigate the Credit Crunch." *Time,* December 11, 2008. http://www.time.com/time/magazine/article/0,9171,1865949,00.html (accessed January 18, 2013).

Kormondy, Edward J. and Kent M. Keith. *Nine University Presidents Who Saved Their Institutions: The Difference in Effective Administration.* Lewiston, NY: The Edwin Mellen Press, 2008.

`Kotter, John P. *What Leaders Really Do*. A Harvard Business Review Book,

1999. http://www.kotterinternational.com/our-principles/change-leadership (accessed February 28, 2013).

Kuh, George D. "Built to Engage: Liberal Arts Colleges and Effective Educational Practice." In American Council of Learned Societies, *Liberal Arts Colleges in American Higher Education: Challenges and Opportunities.* Occasional Paper #59, 2005: 122-150.

Lazerson, Marvin. "The Disappointment of Success: Higher Education after World War II." In *The History of Higher Education*, 3rd ed., eds. Harold S. Wechsler, Lester F. Goodchild, and Linda Eisenmann: 792-800. Boston, MA: Pearson Custom Publishing, 2007.

Levine, Arthur and Diane Dean. "Today's Students: Same as Always, but More So." *Chronicle of Higher Education*, September 10, 2012. http:chronicle.com/article/Todays-Students-Same-as/134234 (accessed February 19, 2013).

Martin, James and James E. Samels & Associates. 2009. *Turnaround: Leading Stressed Colleges and Universities to Excellence.* Baltimore, MD: Johns Hopkins University Press.

Mayhew, Lewis B. *Surviving the Eighties: Strategies and Procedures for Solving Fiscal and Enrollment Problems.* San Francisco: Jossey-Bass, 1980. Quoted in Thelin, John R. *A History of American Higher Education.* Baltimore, MD:Johns Hopkins University Press, 2004. 319.

Miller, Thomas. "Speak Your Piece: Proximity Matters." *Daily Yonder*, November 7, 2012. http://www.dailyyonder.com/speak-your-piece-proximity-matters/2012/11/07/4914 (accessed November 13, 2012).

MSNBC. "Dozens Rally for Student Expelled for Being Gay." 2006. http://www.msnbc.msn.com/id/31066137/media-kit/http://g.msn.com/AIPRIV/en-us (accessed December 10, 2012).

Panas, Jerold. *Board Room Verities: A Celebration of Trusteeship with Some Guides and Techniques to Govern By.* No Publisher, 2012.

Pascarella. Ernest T. and Patrick T. Terenzini. "Alumni Study for the Appalachian College Association," 2001.

Pearson Education, Inc. "What Presidents Think: A 2013 Survey of Four-Year College Presidents." *Chronicle of Higher Education*, March 13, 2013. http://www.chronicle.com/WhatPresidentsThink_Pearson2013. pdf (accessed May 1, 2013).

Pierce, Susan Resneck. *On Being Presidential: A Guide for College and University Leaders.* San Francisco, CA: Jossey-Bass, 2012.

Southern Education Foundation (SEF). *The Worst of Times: Extreme Poverty in the United States, 2009. Atlanta, GA: SEF, 2010.*

Sulfridge, Adam. "UC Officials Mum about Turning Choir Away." Corbin *Times-Tribune.* July 9, 2009. http://thetimestribune.com/local/ x1048573922/UC-officials-mum-about-turning-choir-away (accessed Dec. 15, 2012).

Summitt, Pat and Sally Jenkins. *Sum It Up: 1,098 Victories, a Couple of Irrelevant Losses, and a Life in Perspective.* New York, NY: Crown Publishing Group, 2013. Kindle edition.

Taylor, James H. and Elizabeth Sue Wake, eds. *A Bright Shining City Set on a Hill: a Centennial History.* Williamsburg, KY: Cumberland College, 1988.

Taylor, James H. "A College President's Perspective of Fund Raising, or A Peek at the President." Speech, National Society of Fund Raising Executives, Lexington, KY. May 20, 1987.

_____. "Development Techniques in a Recessionary Economy." *The Southern Baptist Educator.* March 8, 1992.

_____. "The Donor Matrix: Recency, Frequency, Amount, Psychographics & Demographics." Lecture, Vanderbilt University, Nashville, TN. April 22, 2000.

_____. "Faith Isn't for the Faint Hearted." Speech, Southern Baptist Colleges and Universities, 1988.

_____. "Faculty/Staff Speech," Williamsburg, KY. August 21, 2009.

_____. Letter to Trustees. February 1, 2010.

_____. Letter to Trustees. March 31, 2010.

_____. Letter to Trustees. October 31, 2010.

_____. "A New Day Dawning." Inauguration Speech. May 2, 1981.

_____. Notes to author. March 25, 2013.

_____. Presentation for Board Meeting. Williamsburg, KY. April 20-21, 1995.

_____. Presentation to Southern Association Reaffirmation Committee, Williamsburg, KY. April 2, 1995.

_____. "Private Higher Education in the 1980s." Speech. March 11, 1981.

_____. A Proposal Respectfully Submitted to Dr. J.M. Boswell and the Cumberland College Board of Trustees, 1979.

_____. Speech for Council of Independent Colleges Meeting. January 6, 2007.

_____. Speech to faculty and administrative staff. N.d.

_____. "Tuition, Finance, and Fund Raising: Issues for Private Institutions." Speech at SACS Meeting, Dallas, TX. December 7, 1992.

"20 Years of Visionary Leadership." Paper celebrating special event, 2001.

University of the Cumberlands. "Annual Assessment Report 2011-2012: Career Services." September 5, 2012.

_____. "Annual Assessment Report 2011-2012: Leadership and Community Service." September 5, 2012.

_____. "Dr. Joe Early Retires." *Cumberland Today*. Summer, 2002: 2.

_____. "In Pursuit of *Vita Abundantior:* The Strategic Plan of the University of the Cumberlands," 2004.

_____. Office of Assessment 2011-2012 Graduate Student Form MAEd, MAT, EdS Code 952 Summary. 2012.

_____. "Our Freshmen Are Good But Our Juniors Are Even Better." *Cumberland Alumni Magazine*. Winter. 2010: 6.

_____. 2011. "*Strategic Plan 2020.*"

_____. *Student Handbook 2005-2006.*

_____. "Whitley Native Becomes First Dean of Student Employment at University of the Cumberlands." Media Release. May 7, 2010.

Vedantam, Shankar. "Elite Colleges Struggle to Recruit Smart, Low-Income Kids," Morning Edition. January 9, 2013. http://www.wlrn.org/people/shankar-vedantam (accessed January 9, 2013).

Waldemire, A. Neilson. *The Endangered Sector.* New York, NY: Columbia University Press, 1979. In Taylor 1981.

Warmoth, Shannon. *Putting Something Back.* Interviews with Jim Taylor. August-December, 2001.

Williamsburg Institute. 1888. Articles of Incorporation. April 8. In Taylor and Wake, 1988.

_____. 1892. Catalogue, 1892-1893. In Taylor and Wake, 1988.

APPENDICES

A—Board of Trustees

B—Presidents

C—Gift Income

D—Budget Information

E—Statement Regarding Controversy

F—Curriculum Changes

G—Enrollments

H—Facilities

Appendix A—University of the Cumberlands Board of Trustees 2013

Mr. Phillip M. Armstrong, Atlanta, GA 30317, Retired, Attorney

Mr. A. Doyle Baker, Lexington, KY 40511, Retired, Kentucky Utilities

Dr. French B. Harmon, Somerset, KY 42501, Pastor

Mr. Bill Gullett, Gallatin, TN 37066, Attorney

Mr. Bill Hacker, Corbin, KY 40702, Retired, Hacker Brothers, Inc. Construction Co.

Dr. Richard Knock, Union, KY 41091, Business & Property Development

Mr. Howard Mann, Corbin, KY 40701, Attorney

Mrs. Maureen Henson, Manchester, KY 40962, Retired School Teacher

Dr. Dave Huff, Corbin, KY 40701. Retired, Huff Pharmacy

Dr. Roland Mullins, Mount Vernon, KY 40456, Health Care Administrator

Dr. Carolyn Petrey, Grayson, GA 30017, Physician

Dr. Charles L. Roesel, Bushnell, FL 33513-8114, Christian Minister

Mr. Paul Steely, Williamsburg, KY 40769, Retired, Paul Steely Ford, Inc.

Dr. John Mark Toby, Somerset, KY 42503, Pastor

Mr. H. Ray Hammons, Jr., Prospect, KY 40059, HRH Capital, LLC

Dr. Tony Hancock, Lexington, KY 40511, Pastor

Dr. Jim Oaks, Chairman, Jacksonville, FL 32225-2634, Retired, Administrator (Railroad) CSX

Mr. Donnie Patrick, Williamsburg, KY 40769, Banker

Mr. Scott Thompson, Oneida, TN 37841, Banker

Mr. Lonnie D. Walden, Secretary, Williamsburg, KY 40769, Retired, Kentucky Farm Bureau

Mr. Jon Westbrook, Vice Chair, Buckner, KY 40010, East & Westbrook Const. Co., Inc.

Dr. Linda D. Booth, Inez, KY 41224. Interstate Lodging, Inc. & Azalea Hall, Inc. DBA Miss Ida's Tea Room

Mrs. Georgetta Gannon, Mount Sterling, KY 40353, CFO, Boneal, Inc.

Dr. Oliver Keith Gannon, Mount Sterling, KY 40353, CEO, Boneal, Inc.

Dr. William David Henard, III, Lexington, KY 40515, Pastor

Mr. J. Hunt Perkins, Lexington, KY 40517, Petroleum Geologist:Owner/President, Petro-Hunt, Inc.

Mr. Donnie Rains, Williamsburg, KY 40769, Retired Teacher

Judge Jerry D. Winchester, Corbin, KY 40701, Retired, Circuit Court Judge

Appendix B—List of Presidents and Years Served

William James Johnson	1889-1890
Edwin Ellsworth Wood	1890-1893
John Newton Prestridge	1893-1897
Edwin Ellsworth Wood	1998-1910
Gorman Jones, Acting President	1910-1912
Edwin Ellsworth Wood	1912-1919
Albert Robinson Evans, Acting President	1919-1921
Charles William Elsey	1921-1925
James Lloyd Creech	1925-1946
James Malcolm Boswell	1947-1980
James Harold Taylor	1980-

Appendix C—Gift Income by Year

	KBC	Private Gifts	Gifts in Kind	F.H.I.T	TOTAL
	UNIVERSITY of THE CUMBERLANDS- Gift Income				
	at year end June 30, 2012				
1980-81	$ 718,774	$ 2,383,469			$ 3,102,243
1981-82	$ 990,207	$ 1,691,879			$ 2,682,086
1982-83	$ 1,101,675	$ 1,691,824			$ 2,793,499
1983-84	$ 1,154,329	$ 2,030,661			$ 3,184,990
1984-85	$ 1,082,005	$ 2,023,915			$ 3,105,920
1985-86	$ 1,131,574	$ 2,523,279			$ 3,654,853
1986-87	$ 1,256,199	$ 3,258,441			$ 4,514,640
1987-88	$ 1,289,199	$ 3,456,524			$ 4,745,723
1988-89	$ 1,297,331	$ 3,701,583			$ 4,998,914
1989-90	$ 1,318,209	$ 6,887,004			$ 8,205,213
1990-91	$ 1,302,972	$ 4,960,946	$ 23,748		$ 6,287,666
1991-92	$ 1,327,495	$ 6,547,649	$2,858,482		$ 10,733,626
1992-93	$ 1,297,680	$ 6,455,150	$ 87,747		$ 7,840,577
1993-94	$ 1,264,791	$ 6,719,823	$ 426,672		$ 8,411,286
1994-95	$ 1,293,200	$ 4,706,066	$ 412,205	$ 3,703,581	$ 10,115,052
1995-96	$ 1,229,692	$ 5,971,092	$ 143,303	$ 5,729,085	$ 13,073,172
1996-97	$ 1,190,013	$ 6,667,357	$1,078,046	$ 362,000	$ 9,297,416
1997-98	$ 1,161,445	$ 6,993,386	$1,852,701		$ 10,007,532
1998-99	$ 1,242,088	$ 10,661,025	$ 319,267	$ 29,430	$ 12,251,810
1999-00	$ 1,180,184	$ 11,619,415	$1,662,093		$ 14,461,692
2000-01	$ 1,304,680	$ 9,678,531	$ 924,095	$ 1,812,106	$ 13,719,412
2001-02	$ 1,227,264	$ 12,317,245	$1,202,231	$ 9,765	$ 14,756,505
2002-03	$ 1,280,829	$ 9,080,943	$1,290,413	$ (25,046)	$ 11,627,139
2003-04	$ 1,291,898	$ 11,459,782	$ 139,149	$ 30,434	$ 12,921,263
2004-05	$ 1,281,948	$ 7,184,025	$ 186,699	$ 60,029	$ 8,712,701
2005-06	$ 1,292,586	$ 9,317,267	$ 32,593	$ 36,390	$ 10,678,836
2006-07	$ 1,335,501	$ 13,465,188	$ 76,514	$ 84,720	$ 14,961,923
2007-08	$ 1,395,056	$ 11,594,866	$ 135,550	$ 16,746	$ 13,142,218
2008-09	$ 1,470,758	$ 5,014,789	$ 36,201	$ 6,000	$ 6,527,748
2009-10	$ 1,465,882	$ 4,911,718	$ 57,579		$ 6,435,179
2010-11	$ 1,492,674	$ 6,057,936	$ 24,005	$ 2,017	$ 7,576,632
2011-12	$ 1,306,988	$ 7,619,468	$ 560,336		$ 9,486,792

Appendix D—Budget Information
Total Endowment and Annunities

UNIVERSITY of THE CUMBERLANDS
Total Assets After Depreciation at year ended 6/30/2012

1980-81	$7,785,382
1981-82	$8,435,846
1982-83	$8,920,556
1983-84	$9,886,708
1984-85	$9,808,914
1985-86	$11,867,698
1986-87	$11,550,712
1987-88	$11,152,465
1988-89	$10,911,440
1989-90	$11,516,321
1990-91	$13,048,818
1991-92	$17,610,641
1992-93	$18,601,993
1993-94	$17,629,258
1994-95	$21,817,510
1995-96	$27,108,487
1996-97	$33,997,847
1997-98	$37,978,211
1998-99	$39,919,712
1999-00	$43,694,061
2000-01	$45,819,254
2001-02	$53,401,856
2002-03	$51,537,073
2003 04	$56,136,923
2004-05	$56,607,588
2005-06	$59,789,171
2006-07	$63,457,991
2007-08	$62,393,633
2008-09	$54,682,732
2009-10	$63,344,943
2010-11	$70,447,055
2011-12	$70,480,126

UNIVERSITY of THE CUMBERLANDS

Unrestricted Budget vs. Actual Expenditures and
Total Revenue at year end June 30, 2012

	Budget Expense	Actual Expense	Actual Revenue
2007-08	28,000,000	27,900,000	28,700,000
2008-09	31,300,000	31,700,000	29,900,000
2009-10	33,400,000	33,400,000	33,500,000
2010-11	36,500,000	36,100,000	36,600,000
2011-12	38,800,000	40,100,000	41,200,000

Debt As Percent Of Assets—2011-12

Debt as a Percent of Total Assets before Depreciation

1980

Debt as a Percent of Total Assets before Depreciation

2012

Debt as a Percent of Total Assets after Depreciation

2012

UNIVERSITY of THE CUMBERLANDS

Total Assets After Depreciation at year ended 6/30/2012

1980-81	$9,021,311
1981-82	$12,072,568
1982-83	$12,802,373
1983-84	$13,648,371
1984-85	$15,696,130
1985-86	$17,975,265
1986-87	$20,406,932
1987-88	$20,813,773
1988-89	$23,555,111
1989-90	$21,379,842
1990-91	$22,703,257
1991-92	$24,433,260
1992-93	$27,813,380
1993-94	$56,131,238
1994-95	$61,583,701
1995-96	$67,743,989
1996-97	$75,182,705
1997-98	$81,711,757
1998-99	$89,884,952
1999-00	$97,843,755
2000-01	$103,454,476
2001-02	$115,397,010
2002-03	$123,877,978
2003-04	$131,270,706
2004-05	$132,077,691
2005-06	$134,896,119
2006-07	$145,180,476
2007-08	$164,848,766
2008-09	$156,506,370
2009-10	$163,715,956
2010-11	$173,767,767
2011-12	$180,605,799

UNIVERSITY of THE CUMBERLANDS

Total Assets Before Depreciation at year ended 6/30/2012

1980-81	$9,021,311
1981-82	$12,072,568
1982-83	$12,802,373
1983-84	$13,648,371
1984-85	$15,696,130
1985-86	$17,975,265
1986-87	$20,406,932
1987-88	$20,813,773
1988-89	$23,555,111
1989-90	$28,410,974
1990-91	$30,542,084
1991-92	$33,139,402
1992-93	$37,421,233
1993-94	$66,817,764
1994-95	$73,615,614
1995-96	$82,672,313
1996-97	$90,111,029
1997-98	$98,190,476
1998-99	$107,996,917
1999-00	$113,939,499
2000-01	$121,272,965
2001-02	$135,050,256
2002-03	$145,445,592
2003-04	$150,445,592
2004-05	$157,026,894
2005-06	$161,340,828
2006-07	$173,553,150
2007-08	$194,158,501
2008-09	$187,986,381
2009-10	$197,464,466
2010-11	$209,934,992
2011-12	$219,126,924

Appendix E—Statement of James Taylor, President University of the Cumberlands

For Release: April 18, 2006

Until now, the University has been unable to participate in the public discussion regarding Jason Johnson. Federal student privacy laws prohibit the University from disclosing records relating to students, including the disciplinary actions of the University.

Today the University and Jason reached an agreement which allows the University to speak, and allows him to complete this semester's course work for full academic credit.

Jason was suspended by the University for violating the University's code of conduct, which clearly states that students should not engage in sex outside of marriage, including homosexual acts, and that students who engage in such conduct may be suspended. We do not spy on our students and we do not put their personal lives under the microscope to find out who may be violating this policy. However, when it is brought to the administration's attention, as it was in Jason's case, that a student may be violating the code of conduct, the University investigates the charges and addresses any violations.

The University's mission is based on a specific set of beliefs and principles rooted in its religious faith. The student code of conduct is designed to recognize and advance those principles. The University's mission, beliefs, and code of conduct for students are not secret—they are well-known to the students who chose to attend the University of the Cumberlands.

Our policy with respect to sex outside of marriage is entirely lawful. No federal, state or local law has been violated. Not everyone likes the University's policy. But the University does not establish policy on the basis of popularity or political correctness; our policies are rooted in the values of the institution.

Jason admitted that he did not share the University's beliefs, nor agree with this part of the code of conduct. After speaking with Jason, the University suspended him. Jason appealed that suspension.

Jason has had an admirable academic career at the University of the Cumberlands. It has never been my desire to see Jason's academic future damaged by this incident. When Jason appealed his suspension, the University worked with Jason to reach an agreement that allows Jason to finish this semester's work and transfer to another institution with his academic record intact. Jason's suspension was rescinded, and Jason is free to pursue his academic career at an institution which has values more in line with his own. The University of the Cumberlands has not changed its code of conduct for students, and we do not plan to change it.

The University admits and welcomes students without regard to race, national origin, age, religion, or disability. The University has both male and female students and works hard to create a campus community which is respectful of both genders, and an environment which develops the students both academically and socially. However, all students who come to the University of the Cumberlands must understand that, regardless of their personal beliefs or opinions, students must comply with the University's code of conduct as long as they are enrolled at the University . . . .

Appendix F—Curriculum Changes
Approved by SACS since 2005-2006

2006
Master of Art in Teaching—Approval 100% online.
Master of Art in Education—Approval 100% online (Biology, Chemistry,
   Physics, Earth Science)

2007
Reaffirmation Approved
Doctorate of Education—Notification
Educational Specialist Degree—Notification

2008
Doctorate of Education—Delayed
Master of Business Administration—Notification
Master of Science Physician Assistant—Notification
Master of Business Administration—Approval
Level Change and Doctorate of Education—Delay
Educational Specialist Degree—Approved
Master of Arts in Professional Counseling—Notification
Master of Arts in Professional Counseling—Approval
Doctorate in Physical Therapy—Notification

2009
Spanish Major—Approval
Criminal Justice Major—Notification and Delay
Level Change—Approval

Doctorate of Education—Approval
Doctorate of Education—Approval 49% online
Master of Science Physician Assistant—Question Deferred
Journalism Major—Notification and Question
Master of Science Physician Assistant—Approval
Master of Arts in Professional Counseling—Approval 49% online

2010
Criminal Justice Major—Approval
Master of Science in Christian Studies—Notification
Master of Science in Christian Studies—Approval 100% online
Doctorate of Physical Therapy—Withdrawn
Master of Business Administration—Approval 100% online
Bachelor in Business Administration—Approval 100% online
PhD in Clinical Psychology—Notification
PhD in Clinical Psychology—Approval
Doctorate of Education—Approval 100% online
Doctorate of Education—Monitoring Report Year 1

2011
Master of Arts in Professional Counseling—Notification 100% online
Master of Arts in Professional Counseling—Approval 100% online
Criminal Justice-Human Service-Psychology Majors—Notification 100%
    online
School of Life Long Learning—Notification
Master of Science Physician Assistant—Sub Change Visit
Master of Science in Justice Administration—Notification
Educational Specialist Degree in School Counseling—Notification

2012
Master of Science Information Systems Security—Notification
School of Life Long Learning—Associate Degrees in Business
Criminal Justice, Human Services, Psychology—Notification
Master of Science Justice Administration—Follow-up Questions
Fifth Year Referral Report—Approval
Master of Science in Justice Administration—Approval
Master of Science Information Systems Security—Approval

Master of Science Physician Assistant Expansion to Northern KY—Notification

Associate Degrees in Business, Criminal Justice, Human Services, Psychology—Approval

Appendix G—Fall Enrollment Figures for Recent Years As of 6/6/2013

	Undergraduate Students	Graduate Students	Total Students
2006	1524	361	1885
2007	1731	494	2245
2008	1753	825	2578
2009	1760	1198	2958
2010	1746	1565	3311
2011	1726	2059	3785
2012	1864	2433	4297

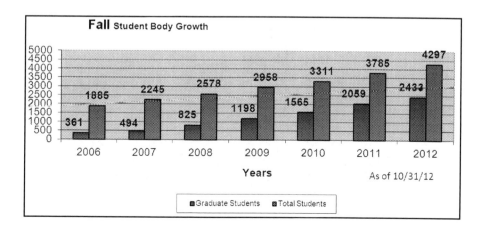

Appendix H—Buildings and Facilities

Angel/Dale House—This building is located on Main Street and houses Baptist Campus Ministries.

Archer Hall—The Ruby Gatliff Archer Memorial Hall is a residence for women located on Main Street, west of the T. J. Roberts Memorial Dining Hall. This residence hall, housing 172 women, was occupied in the fall of 1966.

Asher Hall—The George M. Asher Memorial Hall is a residence for women located on Main Street, west of Hutton Hall. This residence hall, housing 156 women, was occupied in the fall of 1976.

Bennett Building—Formerly known as the Gray Brick Building, this two story brick structure is the oldest academic building on campus and was acquired in 1906 with the purchase of Highland College. It is located on the south hill of campus, adjacent to the Gatliff Building. The English Department, the History and Political Science Department, and the Missions and Ministry Department are housed in this building. Following renovations, the building has been named in honor of Clyde V. and Patricia Bennett.

Bock Building—The campus welcome center and surrounding entranceway were constructed in 1988 in memory of Anna M. Bock with financial assistance received from Mrs. Bock's daughter-in-law, Mrs. Maxine Bock, through the George W. Bock Charitable Trust. It houses the Department of Safety and Securty, as well as the campus switchboard.

Boswell Campus Center—The University's community center, which opened in February, 1972, is named to honor the former president and his wife. This brick, glass, and cast panel building consists of two full levels and one-half of a third level on the back side. The street level houses a lobby, a complex of offices, a complete kitchen, the Cyber Net Cafe, a conference room, and rest rooms. The middle level houses the Post Office, Barnes & Noble Bookstore, and Student Government offices. The lower level houses a recreation and game room and the Campus Activity Board office.

Browning Building—The two-story building houses the Office of Multimedia and Athletic Services.

Browning Annex—This building houses the Student Health Clinic.

Buhl Stadium—Named in honor of Doyle Buhl, this stadium is located on Eleventh Street and was completed in the fall of 2000. The facility includes dugout/locker facilities, a press box, a concession stand and seating areas.

Cook Hall—Formerly known as West Hall, this residence hall for men was completed in 1965. Following renovations, the building was named to honor Jim and Joan Cook. The building includes an office, and a lobby area with individual sections of sleeping rooms that share a common hallway and restroom facility.

Cordell House—This property houses the Intensive English Program, as well as offices for Church Relations and International Students.

Correll Science Complex—The Correll Science Complex is the latest addition to the University's academic buildings. After major multi-year renovations of the former Chemistry and Biology Building, including the **Terry & Marion Forcht Medical Wing**, an addition modeled after Thomas Jefferson's Monticello was opened in January 2009. The combined spaces of the Correll Science Complex currently house the departments of Chemistry, Biology, Mathematics and Physics, and Physician Assistant Studies.

Cumberland Inn, Museum, & Center for Leadership Studies—The Cumberland Museum opened during the summer of 1992. It houses a variety of collections including the Henkelmann Life Science Collection, the Williams Cross Collection, the Dehoney Wildlife Collection and the Rodney Lee African Collection. The Cumberland Inn, Patriot Steakhouse and Center for Leadership Studies opened in the spring of 1994, with additional rooms available during the spring of 1995. A total of 50 rooms and suites are available. The Center for Leadership Studies contains three large rooms for workshops and conferences. In addition, these are used regularly for banquets and special events. The Patriot Steakhouse seats 80 in a university decor. The lobby and grand staircase connect all of the Inn. The lobby includes two huge fireplaces and a special dome.

Dining Hall—The T. J. Roberts Memorial Dining Hall is a thoroughly modern building housing a dining area, reception room, a well-equipped kitchen, and an atrium. The atrium allows more seating as well as a brighter and more relaxing atmosphere for the students. With the self-serve dining, around 1,200 may dine over a two-hour period.

E. Taylor House—This property provides space for athletic offices.

Faulkner House—This facility houses Graduate Admissions and Allied Offices.

Fields/Courts—Designated areas on campus include the band field, intramural field, soccer field, and tennis courts.

Gatliff Building—The Dr. Ancil Gatliff Memorial Building is a red brick structure with classical columns. Situated on a high hill, it has a tall white tower, which, illuminated at night, is a campus landmark that can be seen for a distance as one approaches the town. The Gatliff Chapel, renovated in 1992, contains beautiful stained glass windows. In the auditorium the upper windows depict the life of Jesus while the lower level windows present the history of the college. The windows in the stairwells are of angels playing mountain dulcimers, and the windows at the front of the entrance way depict the University and its outreach to the area. Above the entrance a small round window serves as a memorial to James H. Taylor, II. In addition to the impressive chapel, the building houses administrative offices and classrooms.

Gillespie Hall—Formerly Johnson Hall, a large three-story brick structure, is a residence hall for women. This residence hall houses 129 women.

Grace Crum Rollins Fine Arts Center—Completed in the fall of 2000, the Fine Arts Center houses offices for the Communication and Theatre Arts Department, a flexible theatre that can seat up to 260 people, general classroom space, production facilities and offices for TV-19 and the campus radio station WCCR.

Harth Hall—The newest residence building on campus, Harth Hall opened in January 2009 and is named in honor of Lenora Fuson Harth. This residence hall houses ninety-six women.

Hutton Hall—This residence hall for women opened in January of 2002 and is named in honor of Edward Hutton. This building provides individual suites of sleeping rooms with a common living area and restroom facility to ninety-six residents plus houses the Emma McPherson Chapel.

Hutton Outreach Center—The Mountain Outreach Office is located at the Hutton Outreach Center.

Hutton School of Business—The Edward L. Hutton School of Business opened in Fall 2004. The two-story building contains approximately 22,500 square feet with 11 classrooms, a lecture hall, a computer lab, nine offices, file room, kitchenette, and vending room.

Intramural Gymnasium—This gymnasium was completed in 1928. It has a main auditorium used for class instruction as well as intramurals, athletic office space, and the Athletic Training Room.

Kleist Hall—This residence hall for men opened in the fall of 2000 and is named in honor of Peter and Eleanore Kleist. This building provides individual suites of sleeping rooms with a common living area and restroom facility to ninety-six residents plus houses the Gheens Chapel.

Library—The Norma Jeanne Perkins Hagan Memorial Library houses more than 146,000 volumes, 806,000 microforms, 3,000 media items and provides access to more than 155,000 ebooks, 6,000 online videos, and 50,000 online periodical titles. The Library Collections include the Main Circulation Collection, the Reference Collection, the Periodicals Collection, the Steele-Reese Appalachian Collection, the Owens Collection, Government Documents, the Oversized Collection, the Media Collection, and the Children's Collection. The Library uses the Library of Congress Classification system. Library holdings may be located electronically on the "UC Cat", which is available online through the University's web page. The Library's web page serves as a gateway to a variety of databases that provide access to online journal articles, books, and videos. Materials not available in the Library's collection can be requested from other libraries through interlibrary loan. The Library is open seven days a week during the fall and spring semesters. Library hours are modified during breaks and summer. Library hours are posted on the Library's web page and on the outside of the building.

Luecker Annex—Acquired through the purchase of the old Williamsburg Independent School, the facility houses the Psychology Department, eight classrooms, faculty offices, and mail room.

Luecker Building—The Luecker Building was purchased in 1983. It was completely renovated and then occupied in 1984. Formerly the old Williamsburg Independent City School, the two-story building now houses the departments of Art, Education, and Health as well as the development offices, and the Art Gallery. In addition, the remodeled gymnasium houses the men's wrestling team.

Mahan Hall—Mahan Hall was erected in 1905, and named in honor of Mr. Edgar C. Mahan of Knoxville, Tennessee. This building houses approximately 145 men.

Moss-Roburn Hall—Moss-Roburn Hall, a three-story brick structure, is the original building constructed in 1888 and known as Williamsburg Institute. Moss-Roburn Hall houses 38 men and the offices of ROTC.

Music Building—The Mary W. McGaw Music Building was occupied in January 1979. The 18,000 square foot facility includes the main office, ten studio-offices, two general music classrooms, a multiple piano laboratory-classroom, an instrumental rehearsal room and opera-musical facility, sixteen practice rooms, a music library, a College Heritage Room and miscellaneous smaller areas.

Nicholson-Jones Building—This is a large three-story brick building, facing the Dr. A. Gatliff Memorial Administration Building. Nicholson-Jones houses the Football Office and Baseball Office.

Perkins House—The Admissions Office is housed in the renovated Norman Perkins House, located on Walnut Street.

President's Home—The Ruby Gatliff Archer President's Home, a brick colonial style building, west of Gillespie Hall on Main Street, was a gift to the college in 1962 by Mrs. Ruby Gatliff Archer. The home, built around 1905, is a replica of the "Kentucky Home" exhibited in the St. Louis, Missouri 1904 World's Fair. Every effort has been made to keep the home as an example of the style, furnishings, and gracious living of the period.

Robinson Hall—Robinson Hall completed in 1963, houses 88 men. The building is named in honor of E.O. Robinson.

O. Wayne Rollins Center—The O. Wayne Rollins Center is the focal point on the University of the Cumberlands campus with over 105,000 square feet of floor space. The main arena, with 1,670 fixed seats, is a magnificent setting for convocation, concerts, basketball and special programs. The space on the floor and the top concourse will allow seating for an additional 1,200 people. The arena area also includes a walking track, a hospitality room, an audio-visual control room, men's and women's varsity basketball dressing rooms, concession area, a game officials room, and various offices for the members of the athletic staff. This area is also wired to broadcast live radio and television. The focal point of the stage area is the 10 foot by 35 foot stained glass window illustrating Cumberland's commitment to God and to the students from the Appalachian region. One of the finest electronic organs in the region, donated by Mr. Tom Raper, is housed on the stage area. The middle level of the O. Wayne Rollins Center contains three classrooms, the mechanical room, storage room and an entrance to the middle level of the older structure. The lower level houses a 25 meter swimming pool, men's and women's dressing areas, the entrance to the football locker room, and the entrance to the weight room.

Siler Hall—A men's dormitory that was completed in July of 1985 and houses approximately 100 men.

Smiddy Learning Resource Center—Named in honor of J. Charles Smiddy, this facility includes the Norma Jean Hagan Perkins Library. Also within the Smiddy Learning Center is the Gibson Distance Learning Center. The Gibson Center is equipped with an AT&T PicturTel interactive video system which provides a land network with any video conference room in the world. The lower level of the Smiddy Center houses faculty offices and classrooms for the Human Services Department, the Academic Resource Center (ARC), the Assessment Office and the Office of Teaching and Learning.

Taylor Stadium—The Jim Taylor II Stadium was constructed in the Summer of 1994. The athletic facilities include a football field, eight-lane track, and football practice field. The Stadium will seat 2,400, with facilities for special guests, press box area, and locker rooms for home and visiting teams. There is parking adjacent to the stadium.

ABOUT THE BOOK

Staying the Course is about a college that many describe as being "the way colleges used to be: beautiful, well-maintained buildings and grounds; caring, capable faculty; administrators who manage frugally and compassionately; a bright, energetic president willing to dedicate his life to assuring a solid future for the institution; and students who study hard and work hard to serve those in need." Still the college struggles to maintain what it has built and to increase its endowment, small by comparison to many private institutions, at the same time it continues to hold tuition low and provide funding to students who, even with Pell grants, need extra help to go to and stay in college. How the college is managing to build a sustainable financial base is described in chapters focusing on the kinds of students who attend, the faculty who teach, the administrators who oversee the multiple programs that support the students and faculty, the trustees who guide the college, and the president who has stayed long enough to see many of his dreams for the college realized, to shape new dreams and to raise the funding that makes those dreams realities. The college still struggles in many ways but its struggles are far less than they would be without the lessons the institution has learned and is offering to other small, private colleges facing similar difficult circumstances. With the many stories about the sad state of higher education today, this book contradicts those stories with its description of how merging the values of the past with the information and strategies available today can enable a small college in a region of poverty and with a population of students with limited financial resources to rise above those threats and limitations to become a model for the future of such institutions.

ABOUT THE AUTHOR

After graduating from Appalachian State University with a B.S. and M.A. in English and from the University of Kentucky with a doctorate in Higher Education, Dr. Brown taught at Ohio University and Eastern Kentucky University and served as conference coordinator for Eastern and for the University of Kentucky. At UK, she helped develop what became an independent organization known as the Appalachian College Association and served 25 years as president of that organization. The experiences she had working with the faculty and administrators of the small, private colleges in Appalachia left her with an understanding of why so many fail and so few thrive despite the competence and commitment of many of the individuals within those institutions. She also came to realize how many major foundations and federal agencies are willing to provide financial assistance to colleges that can show promising efforts toward building a sustainable financial base all the while they are providing a strong liberal arts education primarily to students with few financial resources. Her concern about the needs of such colleges led her to write three books about their strengths and weaknesses. The first two, *Changing Course* and *Cautionary Tales*, were published by Jossey-Bass (2011) and Stylus (2012), respectively. Those focus on colleges that had closed or come close to closing. Her newest work focuses on one small college that offers lessons that could prove valuable to colleges struggling to build a solid future despite the disadvantages they face as a result of their locations, current national economic issues, and the growing population of poor students. Between books, she consults with individual private colleges and non-profit organizations to help shape their fund-raising efforts. In recognition of her contributions to this important segment of higher education she has received numerous awards, including six honorary degrees.